S0-AYI-379

Tis The Gift To Be Simple

All the Teachings of Jesus
in Two Parables
and a Dozen Sayings

©2012 Jonathan Huntress

All rights reserved. Printed in the United States of America. No part of this book may be used or reproduced in any manner without written permission except for brief quotations for review purposes only.

Cover design by NRK Designs, Bokeelia, Florida

Irie Books
12699 Cristi Way
Bokeelia, Florida 33922

ISBN 10: 1-61720-377-7
ISBN 13: 978-1-61720-377-0

First Edition

10 9 8 7 6 5 4 3 2 1

Tis The Gift To Be Simple

All the Teachings of Jesus
in Two Parables
and a Dozen Sayings

Jonathan Huntress

CONTENTS

Simple Gifts

Shaker hymn by Elder Joseph Brackett, 1848

Tis the gift to be simple,
Tis the gift to be free,
Tis the gift to come down where we ought to be,
And when we find ourselves in the place just right,
Twill be in the valley of love and delight.

When true simplicity is gained,
To bow and to bend we shan't be ashamed.
To turn around, turn will be our delight,
Til by turning, turning we come round right

Tis the gift to be loved and that love to return,
Tis the gift to be taught and a richer gift to learn,
And when we expect of others what we try to live each day,
Then we'll all live together and we'll all learn to say,

When true simplicity is gained,
To bow and to bend we shan't be ashamed.
To turn around, turn will be our delight,
Til by turning, turning we come round right

Tis the gift to have friends and a true friend to be,
Tis the gift to think of others not to only think of *me*,
And when we hear what others really think and really feel,
Then we'll all live together with a love that is real.

When true simplicity is gained,
To bow and to bend we shan't be ashamed.
To turn around, turn will be our delight,
Til we come to the valley of love and delight

Foreword

Two thousand years ago, around 35 AD, some people on the eastern fringe of the Roman Empire began to radically change their behavior. While there were attempts to stop them, the contagion spread quickly. Accounts of this do not exist in any written record except the New Testament but we can assume that the biblical narrative is essentially correct in the basic details because of recorded events that happened thirty years later.

In 64 AD there was a great fire in Rome that destroyed much of the city. The Emperor Nero blamed the Christians, a new religious sect. That there were enough Christians in Rome to be labeled scapegoats only three decades after the crucifixion shows how fast this new movement was growing. Some of the beliefs of this new sect seem to flout Roman traditions. Several Caesars tried to wipe out the Christians but less than 250 years later, Christianity became the official religion of Rome.

But how similar are the mainstream institutions and beliefs we have today to what Jesus taught? Is what they tell us now close to what he taught back then? Jesus spoke of an intimate relationship that each person can have with God but for the past 2000 years, priests and pastors have often claimed they and the churches they represent are the necessary special intermediaries between people and God.

Jesus was not particular about the people he addressed. He talked to anyone of any class, Jew, Samaritan, Roman, Zealot, or Pharisee. He even talked to women and allowed them into his inner circle which was a unheard of for the time. He also condemned the collection of money and the selling of religious rites to the people.

There are countless books about Jesus, some written by scholars, many more by pastors and priests and some by people who hold no religious office. All the authors find themselves limited by the confines of the New Testament. There has never been universal agreement on what it says, and less so now than ever before. Using the Bible, any author can maintain just about any point of view, and site scripture for validation. The biblical scholars can go into great detail and draw large conclusions over the smallest of arguments.

Theology is a tangled web, and it always has been. Many popular books are based on the author's own religious experience, rather than on historical sources. Experience counts more than scholarship because even the most intense study and scholastic learning can't produce a miracle. But the miracles still happen today, and they happen to people from all different religions and even to those with no religion at all. Why do you suppose this is? Could it be that Jesus has no favorites among the children of God? Which church is really his? I experienced the first of my own miracles when I was still calling myself an atheist. It was quite confusing to me.

This book presents reasonable and useful explanations of the teachings of Jesus. It also shows why they got so convoluted and complicated. The people who saw Jesus witnessed miracles he and the disciples performed. They had their eyes open and their minds followed. An open mind is still needed today. I have tried to show where our modern knowledge is helpful and also where it interferes with understanding the basic lessons Jesus taught.

Jesus 101

No one knows the exact dates of Jesus' birth and death. Scholars think he was born between 6 and 4 BC and died sometime between 28 and 36 AD. Jesus' ministry lasted from one to three years depending on whose opinion you read. I think three years is more likely. The evidence in the gospels is vague but I think it would have taken at least two years and probably three to turn simple fishermen like Peter and his brother into disciples able to speak fearlessly on their own about the teachings of Jesus.

Jesus began his ministry after he was baptized by John the Baptist in the River Jordan. Then he chose his disciples and spent the rest of his life crisscrossing Israel, talking, listening, teaching and healing.

Most of Jesus' followers were common people. He talked in synagogues and to small and large groups gathered outside. Many people sought him out. The religious leaders probably took notice of him soon after his ministry began because word of miracles always attracts a lot of attention. Also, he was seen by many as the successor to John the Baptist, who had been imprisoned and executed by Herod Antipas. Both the Jewish and Roman authorities would have considered Jesus a threat from the beginning. Then and now, authorities see new popular movements as threatening. The people of the ancient world respected ancestry and tradition. The Romans considered any new movement heretical and potentially dangerous simply because it was new and lacked the legitimacy of ancestry.

Word of mouth is an efficient way to transfer information. In the past people had long distances to travel and walking was the only way to get there, but it still only took a few days for important gossip to travel the length and breadth of the land. We think we have an advantage today because our information travels at the speed of light, but it wasn't that much different then. Israel is located at the crossroads of empires and everyone who traveled had news. It wouldn't have taken long for word to get around that there was a new teacher with a new message.

Jesus told the same stories and said the same things, over and over to different groups of people. According to scholars, the gospels weren't written down until at least two decades after the resurrection and perhaps even longer. By that time, stories of Jesus were being told second, third and fourth hand all over the Roman Empire from Egypt to Britain.

There are thousands of books about Jesus. Everything in the New Testament has been examined, dissected and discussed in minute detail. A lifetime is not long enough to cover everything written about Jesus and what happened in Israel 2000 years ago. There are "problems" within the gospels that make a consistent picture difficult to obtain. Some of the stories seem to conflict with each other. The timelines often don't match and things described in one gospel are omitted in another. Scholars work with these discrepancies and try to explain them. Different authorities use different criteria and come to different conclusions. There are hundreds of separate Christian denominations and a wide disparity in belief. There are good reasons why people can't come to an agreement on what to believe about what actually happened with Jesus' ministry.

Uniformity in belief is almost impossible because of the human condition. We do not agree on much of anything. We also think differences in belief are important. We think we are right in our beliefs (otherwise we wouldn't hold them), and we view those with contrary beliefs as wrong or misguided. Throughout history, whenever someone or some group had majority opinion or the power of the state or church behind them, they tried to enforce their beliefs on others. But when belief is coerced, of course, only the outward expression of belief can be monitored and judged. Inner thoughts can't be policed. This was always a frustrating condition for the authorities, which is why in the past the Church resorted to torture in an effort to uncover heresy and make their version of the truth uniform. Torture never works and is the polar opposite of everything Jesus taught. When the civil authorities in Europe finally became strong enough to force the Church to stop torturing women to discover if they were witches, all confessions of witchcraft immediately ended.

The people who personally heard Jesus talk had no access to writings or any other authority to help them deepen their understanding. He didn't tell them to study scripture. No other external religious authority was needed. Jesus talked; they listened. He told them everything they needed to know. He also told them that the resources they needed existed within themselves when he said, "*Your* faith has healed you." Most of his teachings were simple enough that anyone could remember the main points.

Jesus hand-picked his disciples from the general population. He chose fishermen, a tax collector, a Zealot (an underground insurgency that fought Roman rule), and various other people, including women. (When you count the women, there were always more than twelve disciples. The Church, early on, decided not to count the women at all.) Many of his followers were from the lower classes and some were definitely considered disreputable. During his ministry he met a few people who impressed him. One woman, whom Jesus met as he was resting by a well, stood clearly outside the boundaries of good society.

Jesus and his disciples came to the town of Sychar in Samaria. Jacob's Well was just outside the town and Jesus rested there while the disciples went into town to find food. A Samaritan woman came to the well to get water and Jesus asked her to draw some for him. The woman told him that he should not ask her to do this since he was a Jew and she, a Samaritan. Jesus talked to her about "living water," then recounted everything wrong she had done. She immediately recognized him as either a prophet or the Messiah and ran into town to tell everyone. The townspeople returned with her to the well and listened to Jesus. The Samaritans invited him to stay with them and teach them. Jesus stayed in Samaria for two days.

At that time, there was no such thing as a "good Samaritan." All Samaritans were considered beyond redemption by the mainstream Jewish community. The antipathy against the Samaritans went all the way back to before the Babylonian Captivity and is still somewhat present today, although there are few Samaritans left. The Samaritans stubbornly refused to accept the religious law and practices followed by the rest of the Jews. Yet, Jesus spoke to them for two days.

It is reasonable to conclude from this that everything we need to know about the human condition and salvation as taught by Jesus can be learned in two days, assuming that we are as intelligent and pious as the average Samaritan of two thousand years ago.

The Jewish people lived within a hostile Roman political structure that didn't respect their beliefs or practices. Their own religious environment demanded strict and scrupulous attention to the details of religious law. Then as now, there were many in the community who made it their business to monitor the behavior and piety of others, and they did not shirk from their mission.

Today most people live in a much more tolerant atmosphere. Despite the talk about "threats" to religious liberties and practices, things are better now in much of the world. Naturally, there are some glaring exceptions, but for the most part, we can follow any teaching we want and we don't have to worry about what various authorities think. However, we still seem to have quite a few people who insist on informing us where we have fallen short, both morally and spiritually. The human condition hasn't changed in 2000 years.

As books go, the New Testament is not long. If you have a red letter edition you can see that Jesus' words could be published in a very small book. We have had to work quite hard to make Christianity as complicated as it is, but it is our nature to create, rank, and judge differences and separations, even when it takes a mental microscope to see them. We think that with careful examination and by following rigorous methods we can come to the truth, yet all we really achieve is more and different explanations of what the truth could be. Our basic approach is in error and has been from the very beginning.

From the earliest days of the Christian movement there were disagreements. Peter and Paul disagreed. As the groups that would eventually become known as Christians formed all over the Roman Empire, questions arose about membership, etiquette, and behavior. If you wanted to follow Jesus did you have to be Jewish first? Did you have to be circumcised? Which religious practices and laws had to be followed and which were optional?

Different interpretations arose and started to coalesce around several areas of belief. It is clear from the books in the New Testament that this process began as soon as the groups formed during the lifetimes of the disciples. The first heretics appeared almost as soon as the disciples began preaching on their own. A heresy is a belief that is at odds with the accepted set of beliefs, but in those early days there was no accepted standard of belief for this new teaching. There were different and conflicting pictures of who this man Jesus was and just what he said, even from those who personally heard him speak.

Witnesses to any event describe it differently. Two people given the same teaching will come to different conclusions. Despite the presumption, uniformity of belief is not really a good thing. It does not and really cannot exist except by the institution of a rigorous process of education and pressure to conform from a group that has enough power to enforce how people should think and act. This force eventually came in the form of a unified Church that became the official religion of the Roman Empire with Emperor Constantine's conversion in 313 AD. There has always been and will always be different interpretations and questions about what Jesus said and how we should interpret his teachings. But getting caught up with these questions is also a mistake.

To bypass almost all of the theological issues and still take what we need from Jesus' message, we need to understand only a few key teachings. Perhaps the two most comprehensive parables are The Prodigal Son and the Good Samaritan. They embody virtually everything Jesus taught. These two stories tell us who we are, who our Father is, and how he thinks of us. They tell us how we got here, where we need to go, and who is our "brother." These parables are basic yet profound and contain almost everything we need to know to guide us in our daily lives. Aside from these parables there are about a dozen of other important things Jesus said about how we should treat others, how to deal with any group, what things of the world are important and what we can ignore, and how to develop the kind of faith we need to better know the love of God.

So why are his simple lessons so hard to learn? Jesus' teachings, while simple, are extremely difficult to apply to what appear to be the unique and different circumstances presented to us each day. For example, people often wish to be a *good Samaritan* and are on the lookout to find and succor poor souls who have fallen among thieves or had other bad luck. It always comes as a surprise to discover *they* are the ones who need to be saved by the Samaritan, and not the other way around.

Also, the most important lessons Jesus taught are exactly opposite to the basic lessons of survival we have all learned from birth. His teachings unravel much of what we learned from our parents and from our education. Jesus could not be considered a liberal or conservative using today's definitions. His teachings, then and now, were radically different from most of the other teachings of the world both spiritual and civil.

Practicing Jesus' teachings puts us in direct opposition with most conventional wisdom. Going against conventional wisdom is always difficult because it is what most people believe. Acceptance by our peers is important to us and is based on similar shared common attributes, practices, and beliefs. We also share many common fears. The words "prudent," "cautious," "conservative," and "careful" all mean that common, shared fears are considered, evaluated, and accepted. People think that those who don't share, or worse, actively flout accepted fears, are ignorant or stupid, and even dangerous. The followers of Jesus were thought to be all of those things.

A deeper difficulty comes from trying to incorporate two completely opposite belief systems at the same time. Conventional wisdom is the normal way of the world and acknowledges and accepts all manner of fear. What Jesus taught does not. In our daily lives, when push comes to shove, we usually side with our fears. Having faith means consciously choosing to step away from fear and the conventional wisdom of our worldly reality. Jesus asked us to do just this and it is no easier today than it was 2000 years ago.

The Good Samaritan: Who is Our Brother?

Most people think the Parable of the Good Samaritan tells us what we should do when we come across people in great need. But the story has a far deeper and more important message.

I mentioned earlier that the Samaritans were not accepted as members of the Jewish community but were hated and ostracized. There were several reasons for this antipathy that go back in time hundreds of years. To understand the feelings at the time of Jesus, we need to cover some of the history of Israel. King David united the tribes of Israel and made Jerusalem his capital about 1000 BC. His son Solomon continued his legacy and built the first temple. This period is called the United Monarchy. Three hundred years later in 597 BC, Babylon invaded and defeated Israel. The Babylonians destroyed the temple Solomon had built and to make sure the people of Israel never rebelled again, most of the Jews were exiled to Babylon. This was called the Babylonian Captivity.

Large scale deportations had happened before and were a common practice for large empires to handle difficult subject peoples. When taken far from their homes and local gods, their social structure broke down. In a few generations they became like everyone else in the area. "God's chosen people in exile" is a repeating theme in the bible and history.

The Lost Ten Tribes of Israel disappeared in this same way about a hundred and fifty years before the Babylonian Captivity. Assyria, located on the upper Tigris River north of Babylon, invaded northern Israel and deported many of the Jews back to Mesopotamia. At that time, Samaria was the administrative center of Northern Israel. The Samaritans and others taken during that deportation couldn't maintain a community strong enough to avoid becoming homogenized into the general population of the Assyrian Empire and were never heard from again.

The Babylonians didn't exile the Samaritans but left them where they were, probably because they weren't considered a threat. It is also possible the Samaritans weren't deported because they claimed to have both Hebrew and Assyrian ancestry, making them near kin to the Babylonians. Present day DNA matching has shown this to be true, which means that the Samaritans probably are the last remaining remnant of the Lost Ten Tribes, which is a tradition from their own folklore.

Unlike the lost tribes, when the Israelites were deported to Babylon they were able to maintain their community. The main thing that helped them was that at some point around this time, probably while they were in exile, they took all the stories and law passed down through oral tradition and accumulated through the different Jewish tribes, and recorded them in a single book making it the standard for all the Jews from all the tribal backgrounds. This book, the Torah, the first five books of the Old Testament, allowed the Jews to continue some of their practices while in exile in Babylon. In this way they maintained their cultural and religious identity.

After spending sixty years in exile there was a change of kings, and the Jews were allowed to return to Israel. This too was a common practice when there was a change of empires or rulers. The new administration would often seek to curry favor with the people by remitting or lessening taxes, easing onerous laws, and allowing resettlement for those who had been deported by the previous rulers. Some of the Samaritan Jews might have gone back to Samaria during one or more previous amnesties.

The Jews who were deported to Babylon returned to Israel, made a start at rebuilding the temple, and re-established the law throughout the land, *except in Samaria.*

The Jews believed that sacrifices to God could only be made at the temple in Jerusalem and all good Jews had to go there. But the Samaritans had their own temple, the base of which can still be seen today, and their own traditional services and rituals, somewhat different from the newly codified practices of the returnees. The Samaritans even had a different commandment in their list of ten. It was the last commandment in the list and said the only temple they would go to was their own. (They made the first commandment in the traditional list a preamble, so there were still ten).

Several hundred years after the return from Babylon, Israel, and most of the rest of the ancient world, was taken over by Alexander the Great. After his untimely death, the conquered lands were split up among his generals. Israel became part of the Seleucid Empire. This is why the books of the New Testament were written in Greek. For all the lands that Alexander conquered, Greek became the second language people needed to know after their native tongue.

The Greek rulers didn't think much of their subjects and tried to wipe out the Jewish religion. Antiochus IV proclaimed himself the incarnation of Zeus and placed his own statue in the temple in Jerusalem. Pigs were sacrificed to him there. He was following the precedent set by Alexander, whose takeover of the ancient world had been so fast and complete and against such odds that many thought he could only be the incarnation of a god. The Jews under the Maccabees revolted, but the Samaritans didn't join in the fight, having worked out an accommodation with the Greeks. This perceived treason by the Samaritans was never forgotten or forgiven. The Maccabees drove the Greeks out achieving political and religious independence by 142 BC. A little later as pay back, they destroyed the Samaritan temple.

There was also an incipient racial context to the feelings about Samaritans. It had been the practice of the Assyrians to repopulate areas that had been emptied with people from other parts of the empire. The "new" Samaritans were settled in the land and began intermarrying with the people who had been left behind. There were probably quite a few of these, as all the new people became Jewish in their beliefs and practices. Although it must be mentioned, in the old days when there were many gods, divine beings were considered to be territorial. If you moved to a new territory, you had to worship and sacrifice to new gods. The Jews were one of the few who did not follow this belief, although it is clear from the book of Exodus, that given the opportunity to choose, many would still rather worship a golden calf.

The story of Jonah and the whale is in the Bible for just this reason. The message is that Yahweh was not like all the other gods. His power and reach were not limited geographically but encompassed the whole world. A lesson Jonah obviously didn't know until he tried to get beyond Yahweh's reach and avoid the fearful task of preaching to the Assyrians, which is what God told him to do. The Assyrians were just about the nastiest people in the ancient world. When they came for you it was a very bad thing. To seek them out was insanity.

The reason there is almost no racial profiling in the Bible is that the people of Biblical times were incapable of thinking in racial terms. This seems to be an extreme statement, but it isn't. The average person of two thousand and more years ago didn't think of racial divisions in society because he saw the world in *family* and *tribal* terms. His family belonged to a tribe and his relatives would be from his own and related tribes. *Tribal* divisions were the way other human beings were classified and the most important distinction. If he wasn't in your tribe or a related tribe, then whatever color his skin happened to be was of no further consequence.

This attitude can be easily seen in how the Greeks thought of other peoples. The Greeks were loyal to their own city states, but still considered all other Greeks to be civilized people, even when they were at war with each other, which was quite often. But everyone else in the world was pagan and considered inferior to the Greeks.

Empires would occasionally arise that sometimes made it necessary to live with and around people from very different tribes and cultures. But as soon as the empires fell, the subject people probably went back to their old ways or went along with whatever new rule was imposed. We saw this same thing happen recently in the Balkans. When the influence of the old Soviet Union failed in the area, all the centuries of old tribal and religious bad feelings came back with a vengeance.

Thus in Jesus' lifetime, the Jewish community considered the Samaritans to be the worst kind of people: apostate Jews who were also treasonous, untrustworthy, and with a compromised tribal ancestry. In fact, many considered the Samaritans to be gentiles, and not Jewish at all. The Samaritans obstinately refused to follow the right interpretation of the Law, but stubbornly held on to their own practices and traditions, even going so far as hindering the progress of Jews traveling to the temple in Jerusalem to pay their dues to God. The Samaritans were hated.

It usually isn't the most foreign people who draw forth our extreme judgment and anger. It is those who are quite like us with only one or two differences. In American history the Mormons were hated and harried out of Missouri and then Illinois because of two things. They practiced polygamy, which was viewed as quite distasteful then as now. But an even bigger problem was that they voted as a bloc and so were politically dominant wherever they settled. This was terrifying to the people who already lived there. (After a mob killed Joseph Smith, the founder of the Mormons in Carthage, Illinois, Brigham Young led his people far away to the Great Salt Lake, where they had no neighbors.)

A similar thing happened more recently in Oregon, when the Indian guru Rajneesh founded his commune in a sparsely populated area near the town of Antelope. The majority of Rajneesh's followers in Oregon were average Americans, but when they tried to take over the county by packing the ballot box, it caused great fear among the local population. It was a very tense time. The local residents had their guns loaded and placed next to their front doors before the Feds stepped in and sent Rajneesh back to India. Without its leaders, the commune dispersed.

We think similarities are important for mutual understanding. We think the more we have in common, the more congruence or compatibility there is, the less conflict and problems we will have, but our experience with religion proves this is not true.

Of the world's major religions, there are three based on the same people, the same history, and the same teachings. These are, in chronological order, Judaism, Christianity, and Islam. The people who claim to follow the teachings of these three should have the most in common and be in basic agreement about the major issues of life, death and the life thereafter, and yet, the strongest believers of each can often barely stand to be in the same room with the others. You can further distill Christianity into Protestant and Catholic, fundamental and liberal, and see the same history and conflicts. The Samaritans would have been perceived similarly.

There were proscriptions in Judaic law for dealing with Samaritans. Touching them was to be avoided which explains why the woman at the well was very surprised when Jesus asked her to give him some water. Once when Jesus sent his disciples off to do something on their own, they walked all the way around Samaria rather than take a shortcut through the region. Samaritans were best avoided in all circumstances.

The main message of the parable of the Good Samaritan is that it tells us who our brother really is.

A man was set upon by thieves and left unconscious and naked in a ditch. Two proper and upstanding men passed him by, for good reason. Most people of that time probably would have acted similarly. Because he was naked, you couldn't tell who he was or where he was from. He was probably unclean.

Jewish religion put great emphasis on maintaining ritual purity. There was a long list of things you could not touch. Dead bodies were unclean, as were women having their periods. (This adds further to the story of the miracle of the woman who touched Jesus' robe and received a healing. She suffered from an "issue," or constant bleeding. This is why she couldn't ask Jesus to heal her. To touch her would make *him* unclean. She thought if she could only touch his robe she could be healed and he would not be tainted. She was healed, but he sensed it and called her out to identify herself anyway, showing that Jesus himself put the importance of people above that of purity.)

Whenever a practicing Jew violated one of the many religious proscriptions, he had to take certain steps to undo the effects of sin. He would make a mental note of the sin and add it to the list of things to take care of the next time he went to Jerusalem and the temple. The temple was the only mechanism in Israel that existed to expiate sins. For an observant Jew, it was the only way to get right with God.

The temple in Jerusalem wasn't anything like the churches and other places of worship we are familiar with today. The experience of going to the temple wasn't like our present day church attendance, either. The temple itself was considered to be a house for Yahweh, the actual place where he held residence. The only people who ever went inside the temple itself were the priests because their jobs took them there. But the temple was only a part of the much larger temple complex of buildings and courts where the temple business was done.

The temple in Jerusalem was, in fact, a large and efficient sacrificial killing machine with stocks of live animals specially bred for sacrifice. A large cadre of priests and scribes were always there to perform the ritual sacrifices which involved slaughtering and then burning parts of the animals. The smoke from the burning would go up to heaven where God could become aware of the sacrifices. The temple actually had stone channels to carry off the small rivers of blood produced every day.

Small animals were cheap. Large animals, such as a calf with no visible imperfections, were very expensive. Only the richest people could afford to buy them. If you had committed a serious sin, you had to spend some serious money to take care of it. You would buy the animal (this is why the money changers were always there) and give it to a priest, who would sacrifice it according to the law. Having paid your obligation to God, you were all right until you sinned again.

Coming back to the parable, imagine you are on your way home, far from the temple. You are right with God, everything is as it should be, and you come around a bend in the road and see a naked man lying unconscious or dead beside the road. What would you do?

The proper Jews passed him by but the Samaritan stopped and went to considerable trouble and expense to make sure the man survived. He picked him up and brought him into town, found an inn that would take him and paid for his lodging and food. He also told the innkeeper that if the healing took longer he would come back and pay that bill too. Who is the man's brother? The Samaritan, of course. But think about what this means for us. Who is our brother?

Our brother is always the Samaritan; the last person we would want to help us, the last person we would want to touch us, the last person we would want to feel obligated to.

We can all think of several people in our lives who fit this picture. We would rather die than have this person help us. These are our Samaritans, biblically mandated to be our brothers. The people we esteem or value the least are the very ones put here on earth to show us what brotherhood really is. According to Jesus, our true brothers are those who we least want to be associated with and who give us the most grief.

I had an experience of this kind, although it took me twenty years to change my mind. When I was in junior high school, I had a particularly disagreeable teacher. He was stern and dour, had no sense of humor, and because he was also the coach for every sport, unavoidable. Eighth and ninth grade is a difficult time for boys and I blamed him for many of my problems. I was very glad to leave him, and junior high, behind. He lived only a few blocks away and if I caught sight of him coming toward me, I would cross the street to avoid him.

Almost twenty years later I reluctantly realized that I was making my living almost exclusively based on what he taught me in those years. I finally decided I needed to let my old grievances go and wrote him a letter telling him what I was doing and thanking him for all the help he had given me. I didn't get a reply for several months. It turned out he had retired and moved to California. He wrote that he was very grateful I had written. I could tell by reading between the lines that mine was probably the only letter from a former student he ever received.

Sometimes it isn't our enemies who cause us the most hardship, it is our friends. President Harding once lamented, "I have no trouble with my enemies. I can take care of my enemies in a fight. But my friends, my goddamned friends, they're the ones who keep me walking the floor at night!"

I had a good friend who was charismatic but difficult to be around. He had an exciting life and special things were always happening to him. I was allowed to be part of his adventures, although he never joined me in the things I did with my own life. His life was romantic while mine was mundane. He often made fun of me in the presence of others, pointing out my shortcomings. I loved being with him because everything seemed more vivid in his presence, but trying to live up to his expectations was toxic. I was starting to have migraines. My wife kept telling me I would be happier if I spent less time with him. Once I was with a deeply spiritual friend and I related the most recent problem I was having with him. I asked her why he was in my life and why being around him was so difficult. This woman looked off into the distance and shut her eyes for a moment, then said, "Blessed is he, who loves you so much, that he has come to this life to play the part of sandpaper on your soul."

Ever after, I only had to recall what she said to see him as my brother and ignore my feelings of rejection. Once I was able to see that he was acting the part of sandpaper, I could make the simple decision to no longer be his block of wood. I didn't need to react fearfully. I had nothing to lose except the illusion of closeness that I never really had with him in the first place.

In the time of Jesus, another definition of the word Samaritan was "enemy." The parable is a reaffirmation that we really do need to love our enemies. We make our enemies. We can unmake them by changing our minds about them. And a further uncomfortable ramification of the parable can be easily seen. The traveler set upon by thieves would have died without the timely help of the Samaritan. So the Samaritan is not just the man's brother, he is actually his savior. Which means that when we attack our enemies, we are, in fact, attacking those who would be our saviors. Now can you begin to see how hard it is to actually follow the teachings of Jesus?

Love Your Enemies?

You have heard it said,, 'An eye for an eye, and a tooth for a tooth.' But I am telling you not to resist a bad person. If someone hits you on the cheek, turn your face and let him hit you again on the other cheek. If someone wants to take your coat, let him have your shirt as well. If someone forces you to carry their burden for one mile, carry it for two miles.

Today, the concept of "an eye for an eye" strikes us as harsh, but it was actually the first great liberalizing of justice. In the ancient world, the concept that the punishment should not exceed the offense was a new idea. Before, retribution for any grievance had no boundaries. "You put out my eye; I kill your whole family." In the old days, when every other tribe in the world was considered *not kin* (and therefore, not even human) drastic retribution was the norm. We still see this in the blood feuds and vendettas that exist among peoples around the world. Some groups are determined to exterminate others, even though the remembered transgressions are either non-existent or centuries old. In many parts of the world, the demand for justice as *merely* "an eye for an eye" is still a far-off hope.

Yet Jesus asks for much more. In asking us not to resist—in fact, to turn the other cheek, offering ourselves up for more punishment—he is saying that we should not even defend ourselves.

And he really did mean that we should not resist, even unto death.

This is a very difficult concept to take in and even harder to practice. Peter, a strong fisherman and used to the rough ways of the waterfront, asked Jesus for a clarification. "How many times do I have to turn my cheek and let him hit me? Seven times?" The answer Jesus gave him was, "Seventy times seven, Peter."

This one lesson of Jesus is negated regularly in schools and churches. I have heard priests, preachers and scholars go to verbal extremes in trying to explain why Jesus didn't really mean what he said when he talked about not defending yourself in a fight. When this teaching is heard in churches it is always immediately followed with a series of disclaimers on how this doesn't mean to not to protect yourself; but it *does* mean that. It is a rare person who believes that not striking back at all is a valid way to behave.

Jesus meant what he said. The sayings and parables perfectly dovetail to show a seamless truth about spiritual work. To really follow Jesus, it is necessary to move beyond every fear you have and to let go of almost all your opinions and beliefs about judgment, blame, fear and punishment. Changing our minds and our beliefs about judgment and blame and losing the fear of being attacked is very hard work.

Why should we not defend ourselves? How can we even conceive of doing it when there are so many thousands of examples of attacks on others that bombard us every day? We need to look at what defense actually is. Defense is, in itself, a form of attack. According to Jesus, all forms of attack must be given up. When we defend ourselves, we form an alliance with fear and it becomes the way we see the world. We try to build a wall around ourselves for our own protection. This does not mean non-violent resistance. This means no resistance at all.

A wall around a city makes the statement that the city needs to be protected and defended. The thinking that walls are necessary for protection is so pervasive that heaven itself is portrayed in literature and music as having tall walls and heavy gates. Walls around us carry the message that we are frail and need constant protection. Fear of attack invites attack. You have probably heard about the way to walk in "bad neighborhoods." One should walk with confidence rather than slinking along fearfully. Muggers are skilled at reading the cues of fear, and usually attack the fearful because they are seen as being easy marks. The same dynamic works in social settings. Bullies go for the weakest because they are fearful themselves and hide behind a charade of strength. Bullies usually cower when their bluff is called and they are unable to make someone fear them. Confident people are seldom the targets of attacks.

Have you ever held your hand out to a strange dog, only to have him snarl and bare his teeth? It means the dog is afraid of you and is making the statement that you are dangerous and can't be trusted. A common response to this display of distrust is anger at the dog! The dog is afraid for some reason and is reacting to that fear. Being branded an attacker—someone who can't be trusted even by a dog—brings forth attack feelings.

I have often heard corporate leaders or managers say they don't want to be feared by their subordinates, they just want to be "respected." Yet they do everything they can to make people fearful. It is a vicious circle of attack and defense, fear and attack. Those who work hardest to achieve power over others hate those who fear them *because they fear them!* Such is the fate of tyrants, no matter how petty. They seek acceptance through the path of fear, which only leads to more fear.

The solution Jesus advocated is to become defenseless. His teachings emphasize that we don't want or need armor to protect ourselves because we are no longer afraid of our brothers and sisters. But becoming defenseless is no easy task. Giving up our fears can take a long time because we have so many. Living our lives teaches us many hard lessons and consequences. We know that not giving in to, or appearing to disagree with, a tyrannical boss can get us fired or demoted. We are afraid of losing our jobs, respect, money, and many other things. But in order to become defenseless, in order to actually do what Jesus said, we have to work on letting go of our fear of consequences.

I read an excellent illustration of this problem in Nevil Shute's autobiography, *Slide Rule*[1]. Shute wrote *A Town Like Alice*, and other books that have been made into popular movies. Shute was an aircraft engineer and owner of an aircraft company in England. He began writing novels to ease the stress of his job. Between the World Wars in the nineteen twenties and thirties there was a lot of experimentation with dirigibles—lighter-than-air ships like blimps, only much bigger with a solid internal structure. The most famous example was the German dirigible Hindenburg that crashed and burned in New Jersey. England made two dirigibles, one constructed by private industry and the other by the government (an early example of the move toward socialism in Great Britain). Shute was in charge of the private venture. He finished his airship first and successfully flew it to Canada and back. (Government inspectors looked over Shute's shoulder during every step of the construction process, yet they never once asked him to review or comment on how their own machine was progressing. Shute heard rumors that it was not going well at all.)

The airship made by the government was hurried to completion in order to fly the Air Minister and his staff to an upcoming air show in India. Carrying almost all the important staff of the Air Ministry, it just made it across the English Channel before crashing in France, killing nearly everyone aboard. Shute wrote that the main problem was that nobody was willing to say no to their superiors, even though they knew they were on the road to a disaster. They blindly followed their instructions from higher up and kept their mouths shut, hoping desperately that their enormous, overweight, underpowered, badly made machine would somehow fly.

In the rare instances when Shute and his colleagues found a civil servant who had the backbone to tell his superiors what they did not want to hear, they would say, "He must have means." Assuming he was a person with family money and didn't have to rely on his job for his living. Shute checked the few examples he knew of and found that this was true. In each case, the bureaucrat who could say no had independent means.

But the answer to having the strength of your convictions isn't having enough money to withstand being fired. We are constantly given the opportunity to decide matters either fearfully or with the strength that comes from an inner sense that we are doing the right thing. Money only gives a false sense of security. It helps for some problems but is of no use at all for many others. Jesus taught that we all need to develop the faith that we are going to be all right, no matter what happens to us in the world. The trick in becoming defenseless is putting our faith in God instead of in our job, or marriage, or any other security of the world. This is hard work because many of the things that will happen to us will not be easy to handle, but difficult and demanding.

A good example is the disciples themselves. They were an average, normal, fearful, confused group of people until after the Resurrection. Only then did they become sure and fearless, practicing the words Jesus had been saying when he was among them. Their behavior was so changed that some Christian scholars point to this one thing as a major proof the Resurrection did occur.

"You have heard it said, you shall love your neighbor, and hate your enemy. But I say to you, love your enemies and pray for those who persecute you."

Perhaps there is no other concept in the New Testament as seemingly insane and at odds with the teaching of the world as the idea of loving one's enemies. Enemies, by definition, are those who are beyond love. Enemies are those who would do you harm if they could get to you. We have to protect ourselves from our enemies. Enemies are evil. How can you love your enemies?

Most people can't and don't even try. Even if they pay lip service to the concept, but actually doing it takes a faith that very few have. At best, some try to follow the nearly futile and dishonest practice of attempting to love the sinner while continuing to hate his sin. I have yet to meet someone who is capable of separating the deed from the doer, so the sinner is also hated as long as he and his sins are seen together. The practice of loving the sinner while hating the sin is dishonest because it paints a thin veneer of piety over an unchanged core of harsh judgment. You can tell that judgment and blame are at the core of this method by how you feel when someone tells you that you are "forgiven." You are likely not very happy or grateful to learn this. In fact, it usually keeps the original conflict intact and even adds to the disagreement.

The forgiver is twice elevated by the exchange. First, he is the better person because he didn't do what the other did; and second, he is now more righteous because he has forgiven the no good wretch. The person forgiven is also aware of the disparity in this social hierarchy and his lower standing, especially if the forgiveness is done in public.

In a local church recently there were two board members who had a heated disagreement about some matter of church policy and tempers flared. Several weeks later, one of the people involved lit a candle during the church service and explained that he had forgiven the situation and the other. When the "other" was informed of this action, it caused a nasty relapse.

If your desire is to keep a disagreement hot, tell the person you have forgiven them. It is a tried and proven way of feeling righteous while continuing the conflict. The angry and aggrieved part of our minds loves to keep a hateful conflict active and ongoing.

We all carry a strong sense of righteous indignation that appears whenever we think we, or those we love, have been wronged. It feels better to accept this and even feed it in times of conflict. I noticed after the towers fell on 9/11, I stopped hearing the question, "What would Jesus do?"

Yet our enemies are the very ones we are to love. You can't love and kill people at the same time. By Jesus' words, we are not even supposed to defend ourselves from a slap in the face or a hard right to the jaw. So what are we to do? It is at this point that we really need to look hard at what we believe and how we can incorporate these beliefs into our lives. If we are truly going to follow Jesus, we cannot continue to ignore or explain away this most important teaching.

What would happen to us if we became defenseless? What if we did nothing about 9/11, but invited the terrorists to come and hit other buildings? This is an example of the kind of question where the problem is within the question itself. There is no right answer to this question, and Jesus' advice can't be used here because it is in the context of the corporate "we."

All of us have become accustomed to thinking that corporations are real. There are so many of them in our lives and we speak of them so often that their *reality* is assumed. Many like to think that we are living in a "Christian nation." But it is clear that no nation could ever follow Jesus' advice and hope to survive. Even the strongest nation in the world would be subject to the weakest if everyone in it "turned the other cheek."

But Jesus wasn't addressing nations. He wasn't addressing any group. He didn't address the corporate "we." His words were always for individuals like you and me. All of the teachings of Jesus apply only to people, not to groups, and this includes all the churches that exist. Only a person can make the decision to become defenseless. Corporate groups such as governments, businesses and other organizations that want to continue to exist and prosper can't afford to become defenseless. No group will ever be free from fear. But individuals can be. You can be.

Jesus pointed out to people how their own thinking put them out of accord with God, and he told them they could change their minds. Jesus taught that we must overcome fear in all forms. Any use of his words to justify fearful thinking of any kind is a continuation of fearful thinking.

One thing that makes this teaching particularly difficult to implement is the "what if?" game we often play. We ask, "*What if* someone breaks into your house? *What if* someone attacks you on the street? Tries to hijack your car with your kids inside? Drags you off into the bushes? Holds a knife to your throat?" We play this game to scare ourselves and others, and it works. We end up afraid and suspicious, and we look at cars and people differently for awhile until we forget the game. But it is only a child's scary game. All we need to do is stop playing. As I learned in the accident when my son died, if something terrible does come your way, nothing you could do to prepare for it will help anyway, so try to stop being afraid of something that hasn't happened and probably never will happen. We shouldn't worry about anything except those things that require an action right now. Bad things will happen. When they do, simply ask for help. After the accident and the loss of my son, I didn't even know how to ask for help, but it was there anyway. And it was more powerful and helpful than anything I could have imagined or found for myself.

As for the "What if?" game, try playing it in reverse. "What if I smiled at that surly, tattooed man and told him his Harley was beautiful? Does it make him happy?" (Yes, it always does.)

We think those who fear us are not to be trusted. We think those who share our fears are smart people and are our friends and allies. But in both cases, fear is the real problem. Fear is the opposite of love, and to find the way to love, we need to let go of fear. Having allies means you also have enemies. To be without fear is to have no enemies. It is the same as having faith. Faith equals love. Fear has no part in this equation. If we want to follow Jesus, we have to question every fear we have. This is another lesson of the crucifixion. If Jesus could meet his trial, scourging, and crucifixion without fear, we should be able to meet the easier circumstances of our own lives with less fear. We have to recognize our fears and turn away from them. We also have to recognize our enemies and turn toward them.

The early followers of Jesus probably did this better than we do today. From the time they decided to follow the new teaching they were persecuted. When the Roman Emperor Nero singled out the Christians as scapegoats for the fire that swept Rome in 64 AD, he killed hundreds of them by feeding them to the lions and making them into human torches to light his garden. (That there were significant numbers of Christians in Rome only 30 years after the crucifixion shows just how successful the word-of-mouth movement had become. At that time Paul's letters were the only written documents in circulation. The stories, history, and parables that would become the gospels were still being orally passed from person to person.)

Many of the early Christians met their fate fearlessly and died without protest—which the Romans had probably never seen before, except from their gladiators whose duty it was to die fighting. Even though they died for the entertainment of others, they fought until they could fight no more. Such a completely atypical reaction to immanent death must have caused many Romans to wonder just what made this movement different. Many of the early followers of Jesus had no fear of death, which shows that they were certain their own experience of dying would probably be the same as Jesus and that they would suffer no permanent harm.

I don't mean to imply it is a good thing to become a martyr. Simply because this was the experience of some of the early Christians does not mean it was in any way a good experience to have. Becoming the object of other peoples' hates and fears and polarizing the general opinion isn't a loving thing to do. Doing anything that increases the level of fear is a mistake. Doing whatever we can to not raise the fear level in others is the better choice. We can see it working around us every day. When we choose to become less fearful, we are helping ourselves and everyone who shares our lives.

Everyone is afraid of something. The people we see as enemies fear just as we do. But they have different fears and in some cases, we are the ones they fear. It should be obvious that making another person fearful as an attempt to force them to change their behavior is not a loving thing to do. Making people fearful is so common because it works so well. It is a good way to raise money for churches which is why you still see so many TV preachers talking about hellfire and damnation. It rallies the "faithful" at political gatherings and motivates them to vote. Fear is used in advertisements to help create a sense of important need in viewers. Fear sells. Fear works. But fear imprisons as it sells and creates a world within us that is completely opposite from the teachings of Jesus. Releasing ourselves from fear is hard work. But at some point, we have to recognize the need and begin the effort.

Forgiving our enemies by seeing them as our own *good Samaritans* is very difficult work. It may be the hardest thing we have to do. But it needs to be done. We have to learn to love our neighbors as ourselves because our enemies are, in fact, our neighbors.

Loving Your Neighbor as Yourself?

One of them asked a question, "Master, which is the greatest commandment in the law?" Jesus said, "You must love the Lord your God with all your heart, with all your soul and with all your mind. This is the greatest and the first commandment. And the second is like it: You must love your neighbor as yourself."

"Love your neighbor as yourself" was originally said by Moses. Jesus repeated it and reaffirmed it with the Golden Rule, *"Do unto others as you would have them do unto you."* Loving God and loving our neighbors as ourselves is the most important thing we can do. In the ancient Greek of the New Testament, the word translated as "neighbor" means "the one closest to you," so "brother" can also be used in this context. In the parable of the Good Samaritan, Jesus asks, "Who is this man's brother?" The point is that we are to love those closest to us and everyone is our brother, even when we don't think they are, or want them to be. The Pharisees in the quote above were trying to trap Jesus into some kind of blasphemy or teaching that they could rebuke. From the beginning, they treated him more as a threat than a prophet, despite signs to the contrary. Unfortunately, this is normal behavior for those people who have positions of authority because they always feel threatened by new or different teachings.

In the gospels, Jesus showed love for people no matter what their position, where they were from, or how they were viewed by the larger society. Several prostitutes came to him. A tax collector, considered to be on the lowest rungs of society, was one of his disciples. Jesus gave special value to those who were not valued by society. And yet, the person who impressed Jesus the most during his ministry wasn't a Jew at all. He was a Roman centurion.

A centurion was a lower ranking Roman military officer, equivalent to the rank of a lieutenant or captain today. He was called a centurion because he was in charge of a hundred men, a "century." This centurion came to Jesus and told him he had a servant who was dying and asked for help. When Jesus said he would go with him, the centurion said it was not necessary; he was not worthy to have Jesus come to his house, (showing that he was aware of and honored the religious proscriptions Jews had for dealing with gentiles). The centurion told Jesus that he was a man given authority over men, and he understood authority. He knew that his orders were carried out without having to see for himself. He recognized Jesus as a man of God with authority from God, so if Jesus just said the word, his servant would be healed.

Jesus marveled at the great faith this man had "...*more faith than any he had seen in all of Israel.*" It made no difference that the man was Roman and part of the heavy yoke of control that so angered the Jewish population. That he was an official of the occupation didn't matter to Jesus at all. He did not ask the centurion to stop any of his Roman duties or resign from the military. He didn't ask him to become a conscientious objector or treat his men or other people differently. He didn't ask him to join his group. The fact that he was a pagan didn't bother Jesus. *The faith the centurion already had was more than enough.*

Just as it was not important that a person be Jewish to hear and understand Jesus back then, it is not necessary now for a person to be a Christian to achieve the same level of faith as the centurion.

The woman at the well was a Samaritan, considered a pariah, but this made no difference to Jesus. Unlike most, Jesus looked upon the Samaritans with the eyes of equality. And after talking with him for a few minutes, she saw him for who he really was.

Jesus met people of many nationalities during his ministry. The Holy Land then as now was a potpourri of peoples. Jesus and his disciples met Egyptians, Greeks, Phoenicians, Romans from around the Empire, people from all parts of the former Persian Empire, and others. He met masters and slaves, servants and soldiers, officials and scribes, prostitutes, priests and paupers. He saw them all as just people. He saw no differences among those seeking help. Nationality and social position made no difference.

But the history of the world can be seen as completely opposite. Seeing your neighbor as *different* from you is the rule in the world. Hundreds of ways have been used to show what the differences are and why they are important. Many of these are enshrined in the books of the Old Testament, and that is why so many people think they are still important. Tribal and behavioral differences were highlighted then, but mankind is always finding new ways to show how other people are different from us.

Racial differences are basically absent from the New Testament. Slavery was an accepted fact of the time, but it was slavery based on circumstance (usually defeat in war or being born a slave) and not on race. In the U.S. before the Civil War, the Bible was often used to support the continuation of slavery. During colonial times and after it was assumed by whites that blacks were inferior, and therefore more suited to be slaves. In the eighteenth and nineteenth centuries, many whites didn't think blacks were even human, but some kind of sub-species.

A dehumanizing process is always used to explain and continue slavery. It is also used to help unify public opinion for going to war. If the "enemy" can be seen as not deserving to be part of the human race, it is much easier to justify killing or enslaving them. When the 1991 war in Iraq started, the Iraq Republican Guards were depicted in the media as storm-trooping barbarians.

To Adolph Hitler, race meant everything. His beliefs, interestingly enough, were based on the general misunderstanding of the recent and quite controversial theory of evolution from Charles Darwin. When *The Origin of the Species* was published in 1859, it took the educated community and the general public by storm. The book said nothing about human society, but some were quick to apply the principles of *natural selection* to human civilization.

Since The Enlightenment, each new trend or development in scientific thinking has prompted those who think and write about the human condition to try to apply the newly discovered scientific or mathematical laws and theories to help explain why we get along so poorly, or predict what we are going to do in the future. None of these attempts has ever been shown to be true, but that doesn't stop the effort. *Social Darwinism* was the label given those who tried to apply the new science to society. It had nothing to do with Charles Darwin at all.

The theory of social Darwinism held that human society can also be seen as an organism that evolves. The phrase *survival of the fittest* sometimes used as another way of saying *natural selection* is actually from the social Darwinist, Herbert Spencer. This theory held a particularly devious siren song for many.

The idea was that if you had prosperity and position, you were more highly evolved than those who didn't, something the rich would very much like to believe back then and now. At the root of this new thinking was the idea that significant evolutionary racial differences existed and were locked into the genetic make-up. Because of this, any effort to achieve short term improvements would do no good. For example, it wouldn't help to give money to the poor because they weren't highly evolved enough to know what to do with it. They would just bear more less-evolved children which would undermine the natural order of society's evolution and actually set it back. It was argued that any form of charity goes against the natural evolution of society and should be stopped.

Although the original proponents of social Darwinism didn't apply it to race, others did. It was a further justification for slavery and later for segregation and miscegenation laws passed to stop the races from mixing. And it was another prejudice that could be heaped on the long-suffering Jews, who were already blamed for anything and everything and now could be labeled as being of a separate and inferior race.

Hitler believed that there was such a thing as an Aryan race and that it was naturally superior to the other races, but that their superiority had been thwarted by the Jews and other less-evolved people. He set about to correct this situation and fifty million people died as a result. He was so committed to his ideas about race that it never occurred to him that technology has always trumped biology and culture. A machine gun shoots no matter who pulls the trigger. The winner of the battle isn't the side that is genetically superior, but the side with the most firepower.

This was a very old lesson that has been proven true many times in history. The crossbow proved to be superior to the English long bow, even though it had less range, less accuracy and wasn't nearly as powerful. It took a dozen years to train a man to use a long bow, whereas you could create an army of crossbowmen from conscripts in just a few weeks. All they had to learn was how to turn a crank and point the gun-like crossbow in the right direction and pull the trigger. After gunpowder was invented, it only took a little longer to teach men how to use the new matchlock guns, and most of that time was used in teaching them how to march in straight lines. (Rank and file marching came in at this point in history in order to make the inaccurate and slowly loading matchlock guns effective in battle. The first rank would all go down on their knees and fire, then turn and march to the back as the second rank fired, and so on. When each soldier got to the back, he would reload as he marched back up to the front. So that tall and short soldiers could take equal sized steps, the *goose step* was invented.)

Hitler ignored any argument or fact that was contrary to his iron view of the world. He thought race was such a determiner of events that he really believed the English (a racially pure people in his view) could not fight alongside Americans (mongrels).

I use this as an extreme example, and you can't get much more extreme than Hitler. Here was a man who hated, and tailored his beliefs to fit his hatred. All of his beliefs about superiority and race have been consigned to the garbage heap where they belong. We are all the same at the DNA level and have come to the point where the entire concept of "race" is becoming meaningless.

The slaves in the American South were freed at the end of the Civil War. It took a hundred more years of segregation, prejudice, violence, and turmoil for blacks to begin to take a more equal place in society. Today, many people don't see color when they look at another person, especially the children in schools. There is less separation and conflict. But this is seemingly a very hard lesson to learn since Jesus spoke emphatically about our basic equality and our inability to judge others two thousand years ago. But the slow process of changing our judgments goes on. Probably the worst examples of man's inhumanity towards others has been within our own living memory.

Gender differences are another issue. Women were finally given the right to vote nationally in 1920, but even today there are those who believe that women are less able than men to do most jobs. Some still consider women to be less than human and would cite scripture to support this view. There are churches that still don't allow women to do anything but listen to the men.

It has taken a long time to change our minds about how we perceive other races. We have a long way to go in changing our minds about gender, but it's exactly the same process. Years from now, our children's children will look back at our time with a degree of shame, that we could have treated women and gays so badly. You can always tell when a minority is being targeted because laws have been passed that specifically prohibit something that the group does or wants.

Jesus saw each person as a weary child of God. We are the ones who see, describe, and rank differences. We decide who is superior and will be exalted, and who is inferior and will be denigrated, and we are always wrong. The teachings of Jesus tell us that we have it backwards. As an illustration, he washed the feet of his disciples himself, an act which made them very uncomfortable.

Whoever wants to be the most important person must take the last place and be a servant to everyone else.

Jesus' teachings made the promise of happiness to people who were downtrodden and poor. He didn't exclude the rich, but he did say they needed to unburden themselves from what they considered to be riches before they could experience the Kingdom of God.

Sell all you have, give it to the poor and follow me.

I think Jesus started the first movement in history that gave special value to the people on the bottom of society, telling them they were as loved by God and as precious as anybody else. Truly, the poor and the poor in spirit know they are in need, whereas the well-to-do often think they are doing just fine. Mother Theresa said the problem with the rich is they don't know how poor they are.

This is another reason why people in positions of wealth and authority have ignored or argued against these teachings, or tried to re-interpret them in such a way that they can continue to hold on to their own wealth. They know what they think they have and how hard they have worked to accomplish their net worth and position, and they don't want to lose any of it. But the gifts of the world are fickle and can be easily lost, while the gifts of God that Jesus spoke of are the only things of true value, *the pearl of great price.* In the parable, to obtain the pearl of great price, the merchant had to sell everything he had. The teachings of Jesus tell us we have to rid ourselves of our investments and judgments in all the things of this world, in order to experience the gifts of God. The man Jesus told to sell everything he had, and give it to the poor, and then join him, couldn't do it. Few could do it today. Divesting ourselves of everything we have takes a great leap of faith. We can see that clearly with the poor hoarders, who find it almost impossible to free themselves from their hoardings, even when it is only garbage.

The reason why it is important to *love our neighbor as ourselves* is that this is a oneness that flows throughout all of humanity.

All the religions of the world acknowledge this oneness, and most work to embrace the concept and articulate the practice. To love our neighbor is to love ourselves, and to hate our neighbor is to hate ourselves. We get what we give. Every time we hurt another, we actually hurt ourselves and the only solution is love. The only way out is to love the very ones we least want to love.

Why is it so hard to do the right thing? Why is love so rare? How did the world get to be such a fearful place? Part of the answer can be found in the book of *Genesis* in the story of how the world began.

The Prodigal Son and the Human Condition

The word *prodigal* means *extravagant.* The word slightly undercuts the impact of this parable, which is probably the most important parable of all. Most scholars prefer to call it the story of The Lost Son, which is closer to its intended meaning. Some think it should be called the parable of The Two Sons, which calls attention to the son who didn't leave. The parable then becomes a lesson in envy. But this view takes even more away from the important parts of this parable.

The story of The Lost Son states how God feels about us. It explains how we got here and how we presently exist in the world. The parable is actually a re-interpretation of The Fall in *Genesis.*

All cultures on earth have a story, a myth, about creation. People often use the word *myth* to describe something fictional but there is usually a truth at the heart of these ancient stories. The myth of The Flood and Noah's Ark is a good example. Most everyone has heard that the Sumerian epic of *Gilgamesh* contains a flood story very similar to the one in the Bible, although it has been dated to a thousand years earlier than Noah. And it isn't the only one. There are dozens of similar flood myths, some complete with arks and animals, from many different cultures. Yet we have found no evidence anywhere of a worldwide flood during recorded (as opposed to oral) human history.

But a huge flood must have happened somewhere, because there are so many remnant stories. It is in the Bible because it was an historical event—somewhere long ago, there was a huge flood, and grandfathers passed the story on to their grandchildren. And that is the only reason why it is in the Bible. It certainly isn't there to tell us anything about God, if the teachings of Jesus are true.

In ancient times, disasters, trials and tribulations were interpreted as manifestations of the wrath of the gods, and the usual reason for the wrath was the failure of the people to follow the gods' demands.

A premise of the biblical story of The Flood is that God so hated all the people in the world that he decided to kill everybody in it except for one special family. This is opposite from everything Jesus taught. We have to be careful in how we interpret our myths.

Myths depict some part of the human drama in a metaphorical way that makes understanding easier. Most creation myths describe a time and place of perfection when God's child or children were in harmony with God. Then something bad happened that brought the time of love and perfection to an end. This is The Fall when Adam and Eve were evicted from the Garden of Eden, and sin and suffering began. Cultures that never had Judeo-Christian or Islamic roots still have similar creation myths. In most of the stories, God's creations break a divine law, which results in banishment or change.

One of the more interesting creation myths I have read is a very old Navajo story I found in one of Tony Hillerman's books. [2] When the Great Spirit created First Man, there was no evil. In the Navajo tradition, in order to turn to evil, a person must break one of two taboos. He must commit incest or murder a close family member. In this ancient myth, First Man, being alone, could do neither. But he figured out a very clever way of first killing, then resurrecting *himself*. In this way he brought evil into himself and the world. I like this myth because it puts the responsibility for the fall from grace not on God or a fallen angel, but on us. The parable of The Lost Son does the same, as I will show.

In the parable, the son demanded and received his inheritance from his father, then set off to find excitement and adventure. He found both and eventually ended up in a pig sty with nothing. He probably spent a long time in the pig sty before he had the idea of returning home. He naturally thought his father would be angry with him and that he would be punished. It would also have been hard for him to go home and admit that everything he had done had been a big mistake. He finally decides to go home despite his fears, reasoning that if he asks for a place beneath his father's lowest servants, it would still be much better than the pig sty. When the lost son is still far off his Father recognizes him and rejoices.

"Hurry! Get the finest clothes and put them on him! Put a ring on his finger and shoes on his feet! Get the fatted calf and prepare it for a feast! We will have a celebration, for this is my son! He was dead, and he is alive again. He was lost, and now he is found!"

The son was expecting rejection and anger, but he received a greater love than he could have ever imagined. Nothing he had done was held against him. He had come back home.

This is the true condition we are in, and it shows the true relationship we have with our Father: limitless love, with no conditions and no blame for anything we have ever done.

The story also explains how this world of sin and imperfection came into existence. The Lost Son was not ordered out of his Father's house because he did something bad. *He left on his own accord* because he thought he had a better idea of how to live. He thought that excitement and adventure were better than the love and acceptance of his real home. He was wrong.

All he had to do was to come to his senses and return home to his Father. The son was afraid to go home. He feared his father because of his guilt over his own mistakes. We don't turn to God for the same reason. We fear God. "God-fearing" traditionally is considered to be the right and proper attitude we should take toward God, but Jesus said otherwise. It is a very old legacy to overcome. In the ancient world, all the gods were to be feared and the best anyone could hope for was to placate them with continual sacrifices. But Jesus even used the equivalent of a child's name for his father, daddy or papa, when he prayed to show us what our true relationship to God is.

In the Old Testament there are many references to God's wrath. The Bible seems to have two Gods, an Old Testament God who is quick to anger and slow to forgive, and a New Testament God who is much nicer. One of my friends had to read through much of the Bible for a college class. In the discussion afterward, the class came to the conclusion that God had matured well!

Of course, the very idea of God maturing is ridiculous. If a god can mature, then he is not God. If God is perfect, then by definition he cannot contain any imperfection. To do so would make him imperfect, a logical impossibility. If God is not perfect, we are back to worshipping Zeus, a very human-like deity one had best hide from. How many of us still think we need to hide from God? In truth, God has not matured, but our understanding of him has, mainly because of what Jesus told us about the nature of God.

I have heard some ministers say that since we were created by God and we get angry, that God must have given us anger as a natural part of our psychological makeup. If God did give us anger, then there is a proper and holy use for anger. This seems reasonable. Most people believe this and want to be angry at the same things that make God angry. But a close look at this reasoning shows that it can't work this way.

Can there be such a thing as perfect anger, or perfect hate? If it is a manifestation of God it would have to be perfect. But anger and hate are both manifestations of fear. God could only have anger and hate if he was afraid of something. This is also a logical impossibility because if God feared anything, then what he feared would be more powerful than he; there would be some aspect of it beyond his control. We tend to anthropomorphize, or give human attributes to many things, including the mental images we hold of our gods. I don't think very many people are able to visualize God and see him without the slightest trace of anger or other negative human characteristics. We are, to a large degree, held prisoner by the childhood experiences we had with our own fathers, none of whom were anywhere near perfect.

There was a good example of this kind of thinking in the comic strip *Calvin and Hobbes* written by Bill Watterson. In the strip, Hobbes, Calvin's alter-ego stuffed tiger, asks Calvin if he believes in God. "I think so," Calvin answers. "Someone's out to get me!"

In the story of The Tower of Babel, as with the story of The Fall, God is portrayed as being jealous of his human creation's possibilities. He makes their lives much harder by banishment from Eden, then he garbles all communication making it more difficult to work together. But jealousy is also a manifestation of fear. To be jealous is to believe you lack something or are in danger of losing something. God cannot be both perfect and imperfect. To be both, or to switch from one to the other, is insanity.

It is clear that insanity exists, and we only know of two conscious entities in the universe, God and humankind. We know we exist—"I think, therefore I am."—Descartes—and most people believe God exists, based on faith and experience. Yet there is insanity all around us. We only have two beings that could be insane. Which one do you think it is?

The Lost Son showed very bad judgment, some would even call him crazy, seeking adventure when he already had everything he could want or need. We are the lost children of God. We need only to recognize that we have been insane looking for God where He is not, and return home.

The admonition to "fear not" appears many times in the Bible. A person without fear does not hate or get angry. We can all think of many instances in our lives where we had the choice to get mad. It isn't an automatic response. When a stranger is angry at us for some small reason, such as not turning on our blinker, or bumping into him in a crowd, we seldom choose to meet his anger with ours. It is a little thing. It happened, now it's over. We only feel our tempers rise when we think that there is an important issue at stake. Because we can choose how we react to *small things*, we have the same choice over *all things*. We can choose not to be angry. And this goes for hate too, because hate is just anger taken to an extreme.

You have heard that it was said to them of old, you shall not kill. But I say to you it is wrong even to be angry with a brother.

Many think that Jesus got angry when he was dealing with the Pharisees or driving the money changers from the Temple and this would be a reasonable conclusion, if we were talking about anybody else. But if Jesus was who he said he was, then he probably wouldn't have gotten angry. If he did, it would have been hypocritical and a denial of his own teaching. When I see him in my mind's eye, turning over the tables of the money changers, he is happy, almost gleeful, doing something that really needed to be done. I feel the same way when I see the sets of the television churches with tables laden heavily with prayer letters that all came with checks which have been removed and already cashed, the televangelists making tearful emotional supplications over the stacks of envelopes and paper. I wish I could rush onto the set and overturn those tables myself. I can assure you that I would not be angry in the process.

But I can understand how anyone seeing such a spectacle would interpret it as anger. Remember that the stories we have about Jesus all came from the disciples and they continued to have problems with their own anger for the rest of their lives, as do we.

God didn't give us anger. It is something we found all by ourselves on our way to the pig sty. Our job isn't to make anger better by moving it from rage to mild irritation. While this would seem to improve the situation, there is no real spiritual growth because if we are irritated, we still have an enemy who irritates us. Enemies, whether we hate them or just find them annoying, are still enemies until they are loved. Anger can't be perfected. It can only be eliminated. Jesus said we need to do that so we need to apply this teaching to all the conflicts in our lives.

I think everyone can think of at least one person in their lives who used to be an enemy, but is now a friend. If it can be done at all, it can be done with everyone. The main reason we have difficulty doing it is we really want our enemies to stay our enemies. It makes us feel justified and righteous to have enemies we can be superior to. This is why truly forgiving one's enemies is a humbling experience but it has to be attempted, if you think the things Jesus said were right. Your enemies will probably never change their minds about you. But you can change the way you think about them. You can stop thinking of them as enemies.

There is no perfect rage, but there is such a thing as perfect love. We can all feel that. Jesus said that God is love, and the parable of The Lost Son illustrates this. We can conceive of perfect love. Most of us have experienced it in some way. We can see it when we look at a happy child or a warm puppy, or any other part of the world seen through the eyes of love and innocence. Everyone has this knowledge of unconditional love. It is what we all want. We know just what it is because we have so rarely received it. I think this innate knowledge of perfect love is the dim memory of our real home and our real Father.

It is an interesting conundrum: everyone wants unconditional love, but so few receive it. Yet each of us knows that we are capable of giving unconditional love if we want to. But we rarely choose to give it, and usually wait to first receive before we commit to love and giving. This isn't really love at all, but *quid pro quo,* a bargain or deal made between two people. If we want to receive unconditional love, we first have to teach ourselves to start giving it without any expectation of receiving it in return.

The parable of The Lost Son points to what we need to do in order to return home. Accept the fact that we have made mistakes in judgment, and decide to leave our current way of *quid pro quo* thinking and get on the road back to our home. What will help us the most is to remember that there is nothing to fear.

Comparing this world to a pig sty or a garbage heap is apt. Nothing works very well here on earth. There is injustice, hatred, suffering on an enormous scale, all wrapped up in a number of generalized fears of the future that include war, global warming, disease, terrorism, declining resources, starvation, and even the possibility of a meteor or comet wiping out everything. The "authorities" tell us all these fears are reasonable and need to be considered. They tell us being aware of fearful things somehow puts us in a position to better deal with them, yet they so burden us with new fears that just remembering all we need to be afraid of is a full-time job.

The parable of The Lost Son has a corollary: the parable of the Lost Sheep. This simple parable can be told in one sentence. Jesus asked,

What shepherd would not search for the one sheep that strayed?

In the parable of The Lost Son, his father's house is a metaphor for heaven. In the parable of The Lost Sheep, the good shepherd searches for the one lost sheep that wandered off. The story is further proof of the loving relationship we have with our Father, and it points out the reassuring fact that he is actively looking for us, and will not give up until we are found. We can see ourselves as lost, but we are being sought. If it is God's will that he find us and bring us home, is it likely he will fail?

One thing that keeps us lost is the belief that the good shepherd only wants to find the *good* sheep. We think that the shepherd only wants to find the bad lost sheep so he can toss them over the cliff. We secretly fear that we may be one of those *not* sought. But the parable is specific. If all the sheep are there but one, he will search until he finds the lost one. All the sheep are good because all the sheep are His. This parable should create a deep sense of relief and peace within us. Somehow, sometime, we will be found, no matter what we do.

Who hasn't had the thought, "I don't belong here?" When you read a story of someone returning home, or hear a song with the same message, do you feel a tug at your heart? I have a picture in my own mind that goes back to when I was very young. I can still see the image of a steam engine with passenger cars traveling along old, seldom used tracks near the university under a long line of trees. It is just before dawn and the train is traveling east, the smoke from its stack rising above the tree line, and it is associated in my mind with the song, *Sentimental Journey*. Every time I think of the picture or hear the song I have a feeling of longing for something that I know is real but that I somehow lost. There is a call for us to return home, to go back to our Father, to find again the love and acceptance and peace that we know in our hearts.

In the Bible, there is a continual refrain of God's chosen people finding themselves in exile in a strange land. These include the story of Moses leading his people out of Egypt, the lost ten tribes forcibly taken to Assyria, and the later Babylonian Captivity. The story of God's people in exile has continued down through the centuries until the present time. It is not hard to see this concept symbolically and to look at our own existence as if we are somehow continuing to be in exile, away from the love and acceptance that is our birthright, which calls only for us to return to our real home. I think everyone has heard the call in one way or another. And there is work that we can do to answer, just as there are many things in the world that keep us from beginning our journey back home.

Government and Politics: Do They Matter?

In Jesus' time there were four main religious sects in Israel: the Pharisees, the Sadducees, the Essenes, and the Zealots. The first three had different ways of interpreting scripture. The goal of the Zealots was more political than religious, although they would have seen no difference between those two words. They were like many terrorists of today. Their one goal, which they pursued with swords, was to end Roman rule and they were absolutely certain that God was on their side.

The teachings of Jesus must have been a great disappointment to the Zealots. They felt certain that ending Roman domination over Israel was right, proper, holy, and overdue. They would not have been satisfied with any solution that involved acceptance or toleration for the occupation forces, let alone love. Some religious sects today are quite similar. They think there is a great imbalance in the world, and God needs their help to set things right. They think that if they can just somehow destroy the nation, group or other religion that is oppressing or opposing them, then everything will be right again and a new dawn of love and peace will finally settle over the world.

Given human nature, this will never happen. The history of the world is the history of one oppressive yoke after another. The names of the empires, nations, and ideologies forcing their will on subject peoples follow in dreary procession from the beginning of civilization to the present. The dream for Israel two thousand years ago was to free itself from Rome, as it had freed itself from the even more anti-Jewish Hellenistic rule two hundred years earlier. But even when Israel was completely in charge of its geographic boundaries, there were still constant problems. To live in this world is to live in constant stress, upheavals and disasters, one after another. We seldom solve problems; they are merely supplanted by more pressing concerns.

When I was in college, I spent a fair amount of time in the library reading thirty and forty year old news magazines. I was surprised to read of issues that were considered to be very serious problems several decades before that didn't exist at all in the world I knew. Many concerns people worried about back then did not come to pass and some issues they dismissed or totally ignored turned into major problems. Shortly after the turn of the last century, the new automobile was hailed as great progress and the end of pollution. In those days, pollution meant mountains of horse manure and millions of flies.

During the time of Jesus Rome was feared, and for good reason. The Romans dealt harshly with people in the Empire who caused trouble, including the Greeks, whom they greatly respected. To understand the futility of fighting Rome, one had only to remember what happened to the great sea empire of Carthage, the Phoenician colony in North Africa. At the beginning of the Punic Wars, Rome had few ships and wasn't very good at fighting at sea. But they learned and innovated quickly. The Romans realized they could not overcome the thousand year maritime advantage held by the Carthaginians so they changed the rules of naval warfare. Rome constructed large ships with wide gangplanks and filled them with soldiers. The Romans simply smashed their ships into the Carthaginian ships and then swarmed over them turning a sea battle into many small land battles fought on the decks of ships.

The Romans were very tough and when angered showed little mercy for their enemies. (Although it must be said, in ancient times mercy was rarely practiced by anybody.) In the Third Punic War when Carthage was finally destroyed, the Romans went house to house and killed almost every man, woman, and child in the city. They left Carthage a ruin and sowed the fields with salt so nothing would ever grow there again.

The Phoenicians were originally from the land of Canaan. Their major cities near Israel were Sidon and Tyre on the Mediterranean coast just a few miles north in what is now Lebanon. Some scholars think the Canaanites and Phoenicians were the same people. There would have been many Phoenicians in the area at the time of Jesus able to tell their sad history with the Romans.

In the time of Jesus, the Jewish authorities were very worried about how their way of life would survive if things got out of hand. The Zealots scaled up their attacks on the Romans in the years after Jesus, drawing more and more people to their side. A succession of dismal emperors in Rome and incompetent local rulers exacerbated the conflict by giving the Jews more reasons to rebel. In 66 AD the Zealots finally started their long simmering rebellion. They failed and the people of Israel lost their way of life, their temple, most of their religious practices, and their land. The unthinkable happened. Everything the authorities had done to prevent these events, including silencing Jesus, had failed.

The authorities in ancient Israel thought they had succeeded in minimizing the effects of Jesus' ministry. Since he talked of brotherly love and peace and forgiving your enemies, probably very few of his followers would have taken either the way of the Zealots or of those opposed to them. When the Romans came to destroy the rebellion, most of the Jews fled before the legions into Jerusalem. The Romans laid siege to the city, broke in, burned the city, and destroyed the temple.

History is full of stories about the end of empires and the destruction of cultures: Babylon, Assyria, the Hittites, the Persians, the Greeks, Phoenicia and Carthage, and then Rome itself. Few situations could be more fearsome than to be trapped behind stone city walls, with a huge, patient, and completely merciless army outside trying to get in.

Belief in the gods' involvement in human affairs was universal in ancient times. Almost everyone believed in prophecy and used oracles, astrology and other means of divination to try to predict the future and to discern what their gods wanted of them. Likewise, everything that happened was thought to be a direct result of the activity of the gods. If a person, group, or nation succeeded, it meant that the gods were pleased and they had done right. If they failed, it meant that the gods were angry and were punishing them for doing something wrong. When the Jewish rebellion was put down and Jerusalem destroyed, it was seen in the ancient world as the repudiation of the Jewish God. Yahweh couldn't have been a very powerful God if he allowed his chosen people to be overcome and displaced. To many of the followers of Jesus who were just beginning to be called Christians, the interpretation was that the destruction of Israel was God's punishment for the execution of Jesus. This interpretation is still believed by many Christians, though from Jesus' own words, it couldn't be more wrong. It is a measure of our cultural insanity that anti-Semitism was and still is so widely believed and practiced, especially from many of those who call themselves Christians. How can a person claim to follow Jesus while hating him, his family, and the disciples who were all Jewish?

Even after 2000 years there is controversy about the death of Jesus and who actually was responsible. Since his dying is seen by most Christians as not only essential for his ministry, but key for the salvation of the world, this continued placement of blame is bewildering. If his death had to occur in order for prophecy to be fulfilled, then why should there be anyone to blame? The fact that Jews are still considered "Christ killers" shows more about the depraved human condition than anything else. That many of the people who have held these views are churchmen in positions of authority tells us a great deal about the real message of many religions. Judas himself played an essential and necessary role in Jesus' ministry, yet even Pope Benedict XVI recently found it necessary to condemn Judas yet again.

We still think that the preservation of our country and our way of life is worth fighting for. We think now, as they did then, that losing what we have under waves of anarchy is the worst thing that could happen. But history has shown us that this very thing will eventually happen again because it has happened to other empires in the past. They all fail, often in blood and fire.

Yet Jesus asks us to turn the other cheek to those who would strike us, and let them strike us again. He tells us that if someone steals our coat, we should also give him our shirt. He said if they demand we carry their burden for a mile, turning us into slaves, we should carry it two miles.

We call being forced to serve others servitude or slavery, yet *choosing* to serve others can be called sainthood. We can choose how we feel about serving. Demands are constantly made on all of us. Some demands are trivial, while others seem momentous. We differentiate among these many demands. Jesus didn't. He taught that carrying another's burden, whether an act of charity or slavery, is holy work. Our job isn't to judge whether the demand is just or unjust; our job is to serve our brothers and sisters, even when they order us instead of asking politely. Most people learn the basics of this lesson when they have children, but choosing to serve others without question or resentment is a daunting proposition.

Jesus promised a reality that was far better than anything we could conceive. I hope I have made it clear it is not possible or even conceivable to turn this world into anything approaching heaven. Any short-term solution—such as getting rid of Roman rule—doesn't help in the long run. The Roman oppression of Israel was much worse than the English rule of the colonies in America. Compared to ancient Israel, the American colonists had little to complain about, yet it was enough for a revolution.

All it takes to start a war is a small spark at the right place and time. But even when we are at peace, things aren't all that peaceful. Jesus' ministry and the first and second Jewish revolts that let to the destruction of Jerusalem and the dispersal of Jews all happened during the *Pax Romana*, the Roman Peace, one of the longest periods of peace in the ancient world.

Almost everyone worries about war, and most of us live with some fear that the small wars will become larger and eventually come to us. We fear war, we long for peace. But what is the *peace* we long for? What if we could have, say, the next three hundred years free from war? Think of what progress we could make in medicine, science, and the arts if we didn't have to worry about spending so much money on defense. But the truth is that even when we have had extended periods of peace we humans made a mess of it.

There was a nation that had peace for that long, and longer. This nation had almost invasion-proof security and a climate so beneficent and mild that three crops could be grown every year from fields that never needed fertilizer. Ancient Egypt was protected geographically on the north by the Mediterranean Sea, on the west and south by the great Sahara Desert, and in the east by the Red Sea. The only way into Egypt was on the thin Gaza Strip, which could be defended by a small army. The Nile flooded every year, enforcing a vacation for all the farmers and renewing the land with fertile soil. It was a picture about as close to an earthly Eden as we will ever see.

And what did the Egyptians do with this Eden and the thousands of years of peace they enjoyed? The temple priesthood developed and promulgated a complicated religion and way of life that worshipped death. When the annual Nile flood came the people labored to build elaborate temples and tombs. Many Egyptians spent their lives getting ready for their death and embalming. They worked hard so they could buy the most expensive funeral they could afford which was viewed as necessary for the afterlife. Their literature and art was static for hundreds of years. Any deviation from the accepted styles was denounced and censured by the temple priests.

If we were given the peace the Egyptians experienced, the peace we think we long for, we would probably also squander it on something that gains us nothing. We are full of conflict and contradictions. It is interesting to note that what is considered some of the world's greatest art, architecture, drama, and philosophy (that of ancient Greece) was created during a time of almost constant war. The Greeks invented most of the forms of government we know today, but never learned how to govern themselves. Few love war, but what we call peace doesn't seem to have lasting benefits either. What can we make of this?

Jesus didn't give any advice on what is the right kind of government. Nor did he take any political stand on the Roman occupation. According to him, the love of God can come to anyone, any time, under any circumstance. Jesus spoke of a solution that would deal with all problems, and that way is not of this world.

To Jesus, nothing in this world is worth fighting for, even peace, and further, *nothing in this world is even worth defending.*

The "pearl of great price" he spoke of has nothing to do with the transitory and illusory *peace* that exists whenever nations are not at war. It has to do with a far deeper and more meaningful peace that is in our hearts. There are few lessons harder to learn than this. All our inclinations tell us that this is nonsense. But this is the path he showed us. At some point, we have to choose to listen.

What Science Does, and Doesn't Tell Us

Even after 150 years, the theory of evolution is still causing religious controversy. Evolution seems to contradict the Bible, but just like Copernicus and Galileo, who contradicted the Bible by putting the sun at the center of our solar system, all the evidence is on the side of the theory. Some people say evolution is only a theory, but they misunderstand the word. In science, a theory is not just an educated guess. A scientific theory is an explanation supported by *all*, or *nearly all* of the observed phenomena, and without any clear evidence that contradicts it. A scientific theory also allows predictions to be verified through later research and discoveries.

The easiest way to disprove a scientific theory is to find one piece of incontrovertible evidence that shows any part of the theory to be wrong. In the case of evolution, that hasn't happened yet. I have heard it said that all biologists are Darwinists. It is the only game in town.

Scientists are supposed to let the evidence determine the conclusion. People who want to disprove evolution scientifically are being dishonest because they violate the first law of science. They start with the outcome they want, then search for the evidence to support that conclusion. The existing scientific body of knowledge can't be used to disprove itself. It says what it says. The reason there is the theory of evolution is because all the science that has been done so far shows it to be true. Trying to disprove evolution using science is like trying to prove to a mathematician that the value of Π is 42. This is a very frustrating state of affairs to many believers who are sure that the Bible is inerrant. They think there must be some subversive reason why the biblical stories can't be proven and many think there is a conspiracy within the scientific community to prove the Bible wrong. There is no conspiracy.

In any case, controversy over the theory of evolution makes no difference to us. Just as in the case of the sun's actual location, it doesn't matter whether the theory of evolution contradicts the Bible or not. Some people get very upset about the seeming contradictions between what science and the Bible say is true because they think that faith will be undermined if the Bible is shown to be in error. That is seldom the case. We came to terms with the sun being at the center of the solar system long ago, and we will eventually come to terms with evolution and any other new discoveries that seem to run contrary to what is in the Bible. We should actually embrace this because Jesus' teachings also seem to contradict parts of the Bible and how we normally think about God and the world. Indeed, his whole ministry can be described as a teaching on how to step away from the traditional and conventional way the world is seen and experienced.

There is one part of the theory of evolution we do need to consider in this light. Interestingly, it's the part that both those who believe in creation and those who believe in evolution agree with. Darwin said that those organisms that are better able to eat the food available in their environment and reproduce will survive, while those organisms that are less able will die out. He labeled this process "natural selection." The social Darwinist concept, "survival of the fittest," is a more graphic description of what goes on in the world we see around us and on the TV nature shows. We all implicitly believe this concept because we see it in action every day.

In the spring, below my window overlooking a bayou, the new baby ducklings follow their mothers. When I first see them there will be six or more ducklings behind their mother, in a ragged line, each trying to keep up with the one ahead. The next day there will be fewer, and the day after that fewer still. The night herons and other predators eat them. The mother with two offspring that survive to become adults is a lucky duck. Natural selection says it is a dog-eat-dog world, and we agree. Alligators, every now and then a big one, are also in the bayou, reminding me that my place in the food chain can change depending on where I choose to stand. There is a sign on the campus of the nearby university that says, *Wildlife On Campus* then follows with *Caution: Some Are Predatory.*

We go to school to learn what is dangerous and what can be trusted. Our parents try to pass on to us what they have learned: "Do this, avoid that. If you continue to act like that, you will be putting yourself in danger. If you do as I have done, you will have a better chance of success." It is better to be strong than weak. When nations and sports teams choose animals to symbolically represent their national and team spirit, they usually choose strong predators such as lions and eagles, and seldom choose animals that fit the definition of meek or gentle such as kittens or lambs.

Yet Jesus said it is the meek who will inherit the earth, and meek is usually seen as a synonym for weak. It is difficult to reconcile Jesus' words with the concept of a "food chain." In this world, everything lives off the death of something else. How can we fit love, compassion, forgiveness, loving our enemies, turning the other cheek and being meek into this equation?

We can't. It is as if there are two completely different worlds. One is our everyday existence fraught with intrigue and danger, and the other is the world described by Jesus, where we are loved and accepted, no matter what we have done in the past. The two worlds can not be reconciled, but according to what Jesus said, we can choose which world we want to experience by stepping away from all things fearful and living in the present. Endlessly circular questions about what things need to be feared should be avoided. They just cause us to become more fearful.

Jesus told us to ignore all the controversy and the questions. *("Don't think about tomorrow.")* He told us not to worry even about where our next meal was coming from. He asked, *"Is life not more than food?"* This one statement from the Sermon on the Mount goes against the most important point of Darwin's concept of survival and continuation of the species. If Jesus is right, all fears and cautions about the dangerous things in our environment are wrong. Remember, if you can disprove any part of a scientific theory, the whole must fall. If Jesus is right, the theory of evolution is wrong. But then, if Jesus is right, almost everything we do, who we think we are and how we think the world operates, is also wrong. Merely to survive is not why we are here. Mere survival actually gains us nothing, according to Jesus.

Science will not give us any answers here because science is the realm of rational thought about natural things. A strong belief in science can subtly work against our spiritual beliefs, however. Science doesn't believe in miracles, and disparages most anecdotal experience. Science is very much like a religion itself, with its own set of rituals, teachings, and its own priesthood. There are many instances of people who give up their faith because science has proven this or that belief to be wrong, or at least, wrong in the way the world is presently seen. No matter what people say about their religious beliefs, almost everyone also shares a strong faith in science which manifests whenever they start their car or get on an airplane.

Most of Jesus' teachings are so different from what the world teaches that they fall solely in the realm of faith. Science will never be able to prove anything to Faith; and Faith will never be able to prove anything to Science. They are two separate worlds that do not meet, except, perhaps, at the cosmic and nano levels.

Einstein was philosophically opposed to quantum theory because it dealt only with probability. His famous quote was, "I do not believe God plays dice with the universe." But even at the quantum level, where all seemed to be chaos, a new symmetry seems to be emerging. It may well be, that studying anything in enough detail leads us to metaphysical truth. In some way the physicists, mathematicians, and mystics are speaking the same language.

There is no proof for faith. And while it is true that one piece of incontrovertible evidence can undo a scientific theory, the opposite is not true. No piece of evidence can undo faith (unless a person bases his faith on something of this world.) There is no proof for faith except the proof we give to ourselves through the experiences we have when we begin to overcome our fears.

We know if a group decided to follow such a teaching and went off into the desert to pray and wait for God to feed them, they would probably all die of starvation. Groups can't work to overcome fears. Groups tend to amplify fears, because the easiest way to influence any group is to play to the fears of its members. *Groups can't have faith.* Only individuals can identify, assess, and then decide to walk away from their fears. When Jesus spoke, his words were for each individual person.

We need to be aware of one of the double-edged swords that science has given us. The scientific method is used for finding proof for things of the world. We learned to believe in science when we did the simple lab experiments in middle and high school and from the TV science and discovery shows we have seen. They tell us that the world can be tested and proofs can be found. Myths can be demolished. Science tells us that there are specific answers for almost all questions. This is an important point to consider because this idea is relatively new, another thing spawned by the Age of Reason and The Enlightenment of the seventeenth and eighteenth centuries.

With a few exceptions, the people of the ancient world did not think this way. Because we implicitly believe that most questions have a *right* answer, we think there is a *right* way to look at all things, and the other ways and explanations are wrong because they can't be proven or shown to be true.

There are many examples of parallel passages in the Bible. These are stories of the same event told twice, with slight variations between the two versions. One example in the Old Testament is the manna from heaven story when the Israelites were following Moses as they wandered in the desert. One version has the manna miraculously falling out of the air. The parallel story has manna appearing in the morning like dew on the bushes. Another example is when Moses parts the waters of the Red Sea. In one story he lifts his staff and the waters part.

In the other passage a wind comes and blows the water aside revealing a way across. The former source prefers a miraculous solution, while the latter tells of a natural, although timely event.

These parallel passages reflect the same stories handed down in the oral tradition for hundreds of years through the different Jewish tribes. When they put together the Torah, they had these stories with minor differences, so how could they choose which ones to use? In their wisdom, they didn't. They included both.

Two different explanations bother us a good deal, because we think that one of the explanations has to be right and the other must be wrong. We think this way because we have been conditioned by our deep grounding in science. If we could go back and ask an ancient Rabbi which passage he thought was true, he would look at us as being quite ignorant and would say, "What does it matter? Both tell the story of God helping his people when they are in need. That is all we need to know."

And that is a profound answer. Science is in the business of asking questions then finding the answers. This is completely opposite to spiritual work. One statement that rings true is, "There are no questions in God." Another way to say the same thing is that God is the answer to all questions. Scientists do not like this kind of answer. They think every question should have a separate answer. People who seek spiritual answers should actually avoid spiritual questions because whenever a question arises, and they arise all the time, the question itself is a mental road block. As long as we are involved with a question, spiritual work gets set aside. So any answer that works for the moment is good enough. The questions will always arise, but the best solution is to dispose of them quickly, and get on with living.

Ignoring questions is a hard task, at first. The troubles of the world call to us a hundred times a day, and each one asks us to respond with an opinion. Those in authority tell us that we are partially responsible for the problems of the world and there are definitely things we can do to make things better, or worse. How did the world get to be in such a mess?

Why Nothing Works

The reason the world doesn't work, according to most Christian doctrines, is because of *Original Sin.* The first sin of Adam and Eve caused them to be banished from the Garden of Eden where everything was perfect. Their error, so to say, is the religious explanation of why sin and suffering exist in the world. *In Adam's fall, we sinned all* —this was the verse under the alphabet letter "A" in an early McGuffey Reader used in American grade schools of the 19th century.

The Calvinists, early protestants who passed some of their legacy on to the Puritans, Baptists and Presbyterians, among others, tended to see salvation as just barely possible for most believers in Christ, and pretty much impossible for the rest of the world. The Calvinist outlook on life, like their chosen raiment, was grey and dour. They were grimly satisfied that the great majority of people who had ever lived would spend eternity in hell. They even argued for the concept of infant damnation, since this was the only possible destination for those un-baptized or not members of the "elect."

Naturally there was a reaction against such thinking. The Age of Reason, which ushered in the Enlightenment, swept Europe with new ideas about science, democracy, and the flowering of human potential. It culminated in, among other things, the establishment of a new form of constitutional representative government in the United States.

The Enlightenment was antagonistic to religion and to the traditional way monarchies and the churches used power. The established churches in England, Spain, France, Italy and Russia were inextricably bound to the state. The church routinely justified the actions of governments, and vice versa. If you broke a law or committed a sin, you were guilty before both groups and if civil law somehow let you off, you could still be condemned by the church. Church and state worked hand in hand.

This was the way things had always been. In the ancient world, religion was the state as well. Questions were submitted to the gods, and the results were assumed to show the gods' favor or disfavor based on how well the people followed their religious duties. The people of Israel thought the same way, but with one God instead of many.

The Enlightenment resulted in a radical change in the relationship between church and state. One of the ideas the Enlightenment attacked was original sin. In its place came the new concept of *tabula rasa* or a "blank slate." Children were seen as blank slates, upon whom society writes what they will become. Generally, this is what we believe today. We see children as innocent and pure, or at least, more innocent and pure than adults.

But if children are born innocent, where does the sin come from? If sin isn't naturally a part of the human condition, then it must come from some aspect of society. This deduction gave rise to the utopian socialist movements, named after the popular novel *Utopia* by Sir Thomas More, which depicted a society where everything worked and people lived in harmony.

The utopian socialists came up with first one then another reason for man's inhumanity toward man, and then tried to create a template for a new society designed to overcome the limitation. At first, civilization itself was seen as the main problem. Cities were where most of the sin was, so maybe cities caused all the trouble. This started the back-to-nature and the Romantic movements in art, music and literature.

Some thought the problem was marriage. There were actually communes in this country in the 1800s where free love was promoted and marriage denied. Others thought the problem was private property, which gave birth to the idea of socialism where all property is held in common. Karl Marx was more specific and said the problem was capital—money itself. If we got rid of money and just traded goods and services according to our needs, then mankind's natural goodness would come forth. Marx thought greed would vanish if there were no outlet for it. He saw industrialism and the incredibly fast rise of capitalism with its huge profits and subjugation of workers as a terrible thing. Revolution was therefore the only solution.

The last years of the twentieth century have seen the absolute failure of communism, although anyone could see that it never worked as it was supposed to, even in the beginning. It was always corrupt. However, the dream of a harmonious commune of people is still believed by many, and for an interesting reason.

The quest for the root problems of society that began with the concept of *tabula rasa* have at their foundation the belief that mankind is essentially good, and that some element in society has polluted us.

Capitalism, on the other hand, maintains that man is essentially greedy (a heightened degree of self-interest), so taking advantage of this can provide a good living for those so inclined. Despite the worldwide failure of communism, many still believe its basic premise and have increased their efforts to implement it or find some system similar to it, even though the original experiments failed. The true believers continue because they *want* to believe that man is essentially good and there must be some way, somehow, to have a society where our essential goodness can come forth. But capitalism leaves little room for that kind of thinking. Communists and other utopian thinkers dislike the idea of capitalism, which insists the human race is basically selfish.

Believers on both sides condemn each other and think the world would be much better if their viewpoint triumphed. This thinking has polarized the world for most of the last century but we are still as far away from living in a utopia as we have ever been.

One "new age" view of why the world doesn't work was borrowed from the religions of the East. We are bound by the law of *karma*. All our transgressions are remembered and addressed through countless centuries of reincarnated existence. Each soul suffers to the extent that it caused suffering in the past. Some believe souls can reincarnate up and down the animal chain, from amoebas to monkeys. Souls are thus reborn from lower to higher forms of life depending on their former existence.

It is difficult to see a loving God in a universe that uses karma to address the balance of good and evil. The God that would subject his children to the wheel of karma may be a just, but is *not* a loving God.

The wish to picture humankind as essentially good did not come, interestingly enough, from Christianity. In the mainline Christian view, all people are sinners, in great need of redemption. This rather bleak summary of human potential was at odds with the push toward humanism that came from the Enlightenment. Since Jesus spoke of love and how much God the Father loves his children, it is hard to see how this dire picture of humanity developed from those dedicated to following his words, but it did.

Many of our country's founding fathers were Deists who were very suspicious of organized religion. That is why the U.S. Constitution has forever separated church and state. Our forefathers witnessed the results of the cozy, cruel and corrupt church and state relations in Europe and they wanted nothing of that sort on this side of the Atlantic.

Deists didn't try to explain why things were bad, they just accepted this as the way of the universe. They had to take the conception of God down several notches, however. God became a *prime mover* that started the universe and then paid no more attention. You can't pray to a prime mover— nothing is listening. Of course, this picture of an impersonal God is at odds with everything Jesus said.

The traditional Christian view is that we are all sinners, doomed by original sin, and we deserve pain and suffering as payback for our sins, past and present. The karmic view is little better, promising eventual enlightenment only through eons of effort. Most explanations of why there is suffering in the world create more questions than answers. It is very difficult to accept any of these explanations and still keep the picture of a loving God who cares for us more than we care for ourselves. Science leaves us with a dog eat dog world where the best we can hope for is to do a little better than the abysmal odds we're given. It would be some comfort if one or more of those Utopian ideas actually worked, but none of them did, even on a small scale.

Some people who deeply care about the state of the world find themselves drawn to one or more of the tempting conspiracy theories that are currently gaining ascendency. Conspiracy theories have been with us for a very long time. But none of them are true. They were invented as plausible reasons why the world doesn't work.

The conspiracy concept makes good box office at the movies, and it has even gotten into theology. Some think the newfound Gnostic Gospels were hidden because they contained the "secret" teachings of Jesus, which he gave only to a select few. There is evidence in those very gospels that for the early Christians some did believe there *had* to be a secret in the teachings in order to explain the miracles, and also why some of the teachings were contrary to what most people thought. Widespread belief in secret teachings was very common at the time because each temple for each god had its own secret initiations, rituals and practices.

All the conspiracy theories are red herrings. There are no secret teachings and there really aren't any secrets. None of them exist because of the simple fact that almost everybody in this world is pretty much like you and me. There are no secret teachings because, let's face it, people can't keep a secret. When all is said and done, people talk. The truth always leaks out eventually.

But at this point we can make a quick summation. All the problems of the world boil down to an excess of fear or a lack of love. If we can consider a spiritual answer for the problems of the world, rather than trying to rely on science, nature or secrets, then we need to consider love to be the key to the solution., and love takes us away from science and supposed proofs, and puts us back in the realm of spirituality.

We ask questions and then argue about the answers. Theology attempts to answer the tough questions of religion but the answers can become very complicated. People have spent lifetimes trying to answer the hard theological questions. At one time the best minds of Christendom were occupied with questions such as these: *How many angels can dance on the point of a pin?* and *Did Adam have a navel?* Behind the questions were different sets of beliefs and ways of seeing the world. Like the Sadducees and Pharisees of old, scholars still debate over which is the right way of looking at God, Jesus, and ourselves.

It is hard to talk about theological concepts and not get into arguments. Our beliefs are myriad and complex. There are serious theological questions and new ones will always arise. Most of the questions reduce to, "Why is there suffering?" Theologians have come up with a logical set for this question, called a *trilemma* (like a dilemma but with three parts).

1. *God is all powerful*

2. *God is all good*

3. *People suffer*

Only two of the above can be true. If people suffer and God is all good, then he cannot be all powerful, because if he was, he would stop the suffering. If God is all powerful and people suffer, then he cannot be all good.

However, if we do accept that God is all good and all powerful, then there must be something wrong with the way we see suffering. You can see how pondering on this too long could make your head hurt, but I will give you my opinion. If Jesus' teachings are true, then the third statement is the weakest.

There is no right way to look at the question of evil and original sin. It is all a briar patch, and no good comes from claiming one point of view is better than another. All the notions of why there is evil and what the human condition really is were started by good people trying to get closer to God. But when these ideas and explanations were promulgated as doctrine the effect was actually less understanding and more confusion.

The answer is either to ignore the question or find an answer that works for you, and then pay no more attention to it. If any answer to the question of suffering works for you, and reminds you that your job is to love your brother as yourself and to shy away from conflict, then it is a good enough answer.

Jesus told us our Father loves us and that we need to love our brothers, even when we disagree. He said it again and again. Agreement or consensus of opinion is not necessary. Love is. We are quite fond of our own opinions, because they are the result of earnest effort and experience. But we need to let them go.

A few months after my son died I learned an important lesson. My wife and I listened to a man giving a talk in Santa Fe. One of the things he said was, *"When has an opinion ever done you any good?"* I knew he was right, though what he said was both counter-intuitive and at odds with how I saw myself and my own deeply cherished opinions.

Generally it is a good idea to ignore any doctrine, teaching, concept or idea that leads you into conflict with those around you, or that makes you feel more fearful and less loved. If you can do this, it makes living with others much easier.

History is Bunk!

I have always loved history. The stories of the ancient civilizations and the tales of heroism from the Greek myths were in the books my parents brought home from the library and read to me when I was young. I switched majors several times in college but I always came back to history. Thus it took me a long time to realize that as far as history goes, one of the wisest men in our own history was Henry Ford, who said, "History is bunk!"

He was ridiculed for that statement, but it is essentially true because history is what historians say it is, and each new generation of historians rewrites the history of the world.

History is not static, but is subject to change and interpretation. Karl Marx changed the study of history by asserting that all history could be seen as a struggle between the class who ruled and those they ruled over. Few historians accepted this view, but they began looking at history differently after Marx, seeing the search for money and economic gain as important influences for events. Other driving factors for historical change have been identified. Going beyond the traditional focus on dynasties, wars, kings and empires, modern historians focus on economic factors, social and ethnic movements, and now even ecology.

The ecological movement is forcing us to see our world differently and this is finding its way into our textbooks. It is another lens we use to better understand how and why things happened even in the far past. Rome, and in fact all cultures before our own, gave little or no thought to the ecological consequences of large numbers of people living in close proximity. The Romans cut down the forests of the Middle East and North Africa, which was the breadbasket of the Empire. What used to be green is now desert and the ancient harbors are silted in. This *desertification* is probably one of the causes that contributed to the decline and fall of the Roman Empire.

During the Cold War in the sixties and seventies many worried about what would happen to our environment if there were a nuclear war. A nuclear war could cause a "nuclear winter," and threaten all life. Dust put into the atmosphere by many bombs would block the sun and cool the earth. Louis Alvarez realized that an asteroid impact would put far more dust into the air than any nuclear exchange and came up with the smoking gun that killed off the dinosaurs. This insight appeared immediately obvious and required that all textbooks that discuss the early history of the earth and extinctions be rewritten. (It also dealt a blow to the idea of natural selection as "progress." What good does it do to evolve to the top of the so-called food chain when every now and then something comes in from outer space and wipes out virtually all life?)

Historians and scholars who write about the time of Jesus and before have very little to go on. Israel was a backwater province of the Roman Empire and few Romans of the time paid it much attention. The earliest gospels we have are copies of copies and written in crude, marketplace Greek without any punctuation or even spaces between words. Some scholars who write about the history of New Testament times base whole lines of argument on a single word or two in the gospels. For example, it is generally believed Jesus was a carpenter who followed the trade of his father before he started his ministry. The original word for carpenter in ancient Greek has been translated by some contemporary scholars as a person who isn't necessarily a woodworker, but someone who works with his hands, meaning Jesus could have been a mason or even a laborer. That particular translation is the only evidence they have for Jesus possibly not being a carpenter. Christian tradition, however, has him as a carpenter. Tradition has roots that are oral, not written. Historians discount oral tradition, but they shouldn't.

We put great emphasis on being literate, but it was a different world two thousand years ago. Very few people could read and write, but they were certainly not ignorant. Almost everything you needed to know could be found by asking the right person. Memory was more important then. Today we can always check the written sources, but back then, they couldn't. This is one reason why swearing an oath carried such weight. An oath was often all you had to depend on.

Most information wasn't kept on papyrus or paper, it existed *in* people. The gospels weren't written down for several decades after Jesus' death but that didn't mean they didn't exist. They existed as oral stories passed from person to person. There were hundreds of people still living who personally heard Jesus, with the original disciples being the best sources, and they would tell you about him. When that generation started to die off, and the followers of Jesus found themselves farther and farther away from Israel, the written gospels, which were written texts of some of the oral stories, often compilations from several different sources, came into being.

In our modern world, as people of the written word, we believe the written word is sacrosanct. We think it is the only accurate way to pass knowledge from one generation to the next. We look upon ourselves as being at the apex of the pyramid of history, standing on the shoulders of all who have come before, and that we have absorbed and eclipsed their accumulated learning. We think we have also been able to learn from their many mistakes but this only cultural snobbery. The people of a hundred years ago thought the same way, and we know how little they actually knew about the world compared to what we know now. A hundred years ago the average man in America was a racist homophobe who believed women to be the lesser of the species totally incapable of doing the same work as men, particularly white men. A hundred years from now, we will be perceived by our descendents in a similar way. There is always a hubris of the present generation that assumes it is the flower of evolution and the culmination of history. We constantly re-write the history of the world, yet we think that the present version of history is accurate. Based on the lessons of the past, this belief has little chance of being true.

Scholars tend to deprecate oral tradition because they assume that it is much easier for errors to creep into the material. But the written word is just as subject to scribal error and deliberate change, and all eyewitness accounts vary according to the witness who sees and hears the events. We don't trust our own memories because we know how easily we can forget things, but this was less the case when memory was all we had.

The creation and flood myths along with the tribal history of peoples were passed down through those special ones who were tasked with remembering. These "wisdom keepers" remembered the legends, and they did a very good job. At various times in history, civilization has taken a step or two backwards. The Middle Ages was one of these times. The learning of the Greeks and Romans was lost in Europe and very few people could read and write, so the oral tradition came back for both historical and legal needs. Epic poems, easier to remember because of rhyme and meter, were created to carry the knowledge and news. The people who remembered could recite an epic poem with several hundred stanzas perfectly after hearing it only two or three times. The human mind is an awesome thing, and if necessary, it can easily do this and more. Nowadays we may hear of such feats only in autistic people, but it is enough to know that the capability exists. It is possible to remember everything we have ever seen or heard or read. I know a person who memorized all of Shakespeare and if you recite a line from any play he can continue it for as long as you are willing to listen.

At some point with each culture, the oral traditions were finally written down, but oral tradition reaches right up to the present time in some places in the world. Paul Ilton was a German journalist and amateur archeologist working in Jerusalem after the First World War when Israel was under British rule after the fall of the Ottoman Empire. In 1925, he went to the tiny Palestinian village of Zorah to dig in some Canaanite ruins. He was followed into the ruins by several young boys, grandsons of the local sheik. Ilton told them of the history of the area going back to the time of the book of Judges. When he got back to the village the sheik invited him to dinner. Ilton asked his host if he knew about Samson, because the Bible held that he was from Zorah. The sheik didn't know, and Ilton began telling the story. He had only just started when the sheik smiled and stopped him and told him of the local man from long ago who had the strength of ten men and could lift a heavy plow with one hand and hold it at arms length. He had the misfortune to fall in love with the wrong woman and came to a bad end because he told her his strength was in his curly hair and she cut it all off one night. This story had been passed to the sheik from his grandfather who had heard it from his grandfather. It had stayed in the oral tradition fairly intact for at least 2000 years and perhaps even 3000. The name of the village, Zorah, means "curly hair" in Arabic, although it was originally an Assyrian word.[3]

One thing I have observed in historical writing and research, is a systematic deprecation of the people in the past. They are often portrayed as simple, unobservant, uncreative, unintelligent and even childlike. They are sometimes portrayed as being afraid of everyday things like thunder and lightning because they didn't know the explanation. Of course, this paternalistic attitude toward the past is completely unjustified. Our ancestors knew their world more intimately than we know our own and were well aware of everything that regularly happened and what they needed to do about it. They would not have been afraid. They weren't stupid, after all. In fact, there is a good chance they were more intuitive and inventive than we are.

When I was working in the prison system as a teacher I was amazed at the ability of many inmates, men who had seldom done well in the public schools, to be able to create the most complicated and ingenious ways to circumvent the rules and difficulties of being incarcerated. These men were in a hostile environment where they were watched all the time and had almost nothing in the way of materials or tools, yet their accomplishments using available supplies and patience (which they never seemed to have when they were in school or on the outside) were nothing short of astounding. Their knowledge, painfully gained and constantly threatened, is also passed on almost exclusively by oral tradition. Prisons are one of the few places left in our society where it continues to exist.

To us the written word is all-important. Our accumulated history and culture is documented by all the written words in all the books. We can check sources to confirm what we need to know, and there is, for better and worse, the internet ark of words which also includes the texts of the ages.

The bottom line is that what we hear from others is "hearsay," untrustworthy in court and most everywhere else. We do not trust words written on air.

In Jesus' time, just like today, there was gossip, foreign news, new teachers, tales of heroism and love, kings and rogues, and always, new things to worry about. Every town, even the small ones, would have "knowledge people" who carried the news. One latter-day remnant is the village gossip, a central character in many old novels. This person wanted to know everything about the neighbors and would visit everyone in town regularly, listen carefully, or not, and then pass the news to everyone else.

I had a great aunt who was one of these people. She died in the 1960s, and her town was large, so she confined her knowledge gathering to those in her extended family. She would visit my grandmother often, and she would poke and pry and nudge until she worked out the tidbit, whatever it was, that she valued. Then she would leave to visit another relative and tell them her new morsel. There are few of these classical gossips left, I think. The towns have become too big and it is so much easier to get a facsimile of gossip from watching the soap operas and tuning in to the constant media coverage of famous people. It is much more interesting nowadays to take an interest in famous peoples' lives, or lack thereof.

Modern day scholars concentrate on a few scraps of parchment, and make deductions based on the smallest evidence, because the rich oral tradition that was the primary source of information is gone. They also make these deductions through a twentieth century filter that makes certain assumptions. For example, most scholars believe the gospels weren't written down until several decades after Jesus died. Some believe, based on this conclusion, that the gospels were *created* at the time they were written, and that much of what we think we know about Jesus was concocted by unknown but very creative people with a specific agenda for wanting the new Christian movement to go in this or that direction. But this is not true.

The gospels, along with the Gnostic gospels, are the remnants of a much larger body of information that was circulating by word of mouth throughout the Roman Empire about this man, Jesus, who lived and died in a small country on the edge of the Empire. Certainly some stories got the point wrong, and some were enhanced in the telling or changed so that this or that point was emphasized in order to address a specific problem for one group or another. I am sure there were many who simply could not believe that Jesus really meant what he said about loving your enemies. I know many Christians today who don't believe that. They much prefer the picture painted by the televangelists of a horse mounted, crown wearing, royally robed Jesus, complete with sword, ready to smite all the unbelievers at the dawning of the second coming. (Don't hold your breath for that!)

However, the stories in the New Testament basically agree with each other. It isn't difficult to see what the main teachings were and are. Don't look for the historians to come up with any earth shaking information about Jesus or biblical times. There will always be new books and new interpretations. Indeed, this is one of them. But historians have very limited sources and fresh material is slow to appear. Even when there are new archeological finds, it doesn't mean that anything will change. We are very resistant to changing our minds. It is probably the hardest thing in the world for us to do.

What about Archaeology?

The science of archaeology is only about 150 years old. The *Iliad*, Homer's epic poem of the Trojan War, was considered by most scholars to be a foundationless myth until Heinrich Schliemann found the actual city of Troy in the 1870s. This and other discoveries started an ongoing love affair with archaeology and the past.

Some people worry about the facts of archaeology and how it can confirm or deny what is written in the Bible. One group of archaeologists, the minimalists, practice a new school of thought. They assert that no old written history can be considered accurate unless it is backed by archaeological discoveries. There are several things wrong with this way of thinking. First, there is little archaeological evidence more than a thousand years old that directly supports any written records. Archaeology deals with bits and pieces and is very limited in what it can tell us of the past. It tells us more about what people ate and what kind of houses they lived in than what they thought.

There are other suspicious things about minimalist thought. For one thing, much of it seems to be centered on discounting or completely eliminating the role of the Jews in history by turning the Bible into a book of fictional legends. The reason for this is unpleasantly obvious. If the Jews have no history, they have no claim on the land they occupy now. It is the newest form of anti-Semitism and because it hides within ivory towers, it is scholastically acceptable, although just barely. Progress in recognizing and denying prejudice, even among intellectuals, is historically slower than glaciers.

Another big problem for archaeology is that the *average* time it takes for a discovery to make it into a scholarly publication is twenty-five years. There are different reasons for this. *The Nag Hamadi Chronicles* (the Gnostic library found in Egypt in 1948) were finally published in the 1970s. It took so long because the books were written in Coptic, and there are only a handful of scholars who know that language.

The Dead Sea Scrolls, found in 1947, took even longer to publish because the team that has sole access to them refused to publish the scrolls themselves. They studied them for years and years, occasionally publishing bits and pieces about the scrolls. This was extremely frustrating for biblical scholars for while many of the scrolls were copies of existing biblical books, there were other scrolls that were unique and were seeing the light for the first time in two thousand years. The scrolls ended up being first published in a completely unexpected way. A secret concordance of the scrolls existed, written only for members of the team, listing where every word existed in all the scrolls. One of the copies of that book was made available to a professor outside the team in the United States, and his graduate assistant realized that if they could input all the information from the concordance into his computer they could digitally reassemble the scrolls. This they did in 1991, and for the first time, *The Dead Sea Scrolls* were actually published. The scrolls team was furious but it was too late. The monopoly had been broken. The intact scrolls have been published, but there is still a large number of fragments that have not yet been put together or published.

Most archaeological excavations have a similarly long time from excavation to publication. Funding is the main problem. With all that is needed in the world, finding the money to dig a hole in the ground where you *might* find something important is difficult. Funding is usually just enough to cover the expenses of an expedition. Everything dug up is classified and saved. Mountains of raw data are collected. After an expedition, the archaeologists return to their universities and their regular teaching schedules, where they have to steal the time to sort through everything and write up their conclusions. This is the part that causes the long wait. Some scholars have died before their results were published, and the data and artifacts they collected are still lying in university basements.

No matter what the trend in scholarship, an average twenty-five year time lapse from discovery to disclosure means that the archaeological record is usually not reliable for confirming or denying anything. Also, archaeologists often undo the work of their predecessors. When the mound of Jericho was first excavated it turned out to be 11,000 years old, one of the oldest cities in the world. The most interesting level to biblical scholars, however, was confirming the Old Testament story of the fall of Jericho when Joshua called on God and "the walls came a-tumbling down." John Garstang dug the city in 1930 and found a layer where the city walls were down and seemed to have all fallen outward. He dated it to the time of Joshua. When Kathleen Kenyon excavated it some twenty years later, she said his dates were off by at least a hundred years and at the time of Joshua there was no existing city on the site at all. In the 1990s another scholar carbon dated the burn layer to redate those walls back to the time of Joshua. However, there was something wrong with his testing and they were dated again to the earlier time that Kenyon had claimed. We still hear about the Garstang dig showing proof the Bible was right, and it might well be. The next dig could switch it back. The history of the world is always changing.

Artifacts from the past continue to bring forth strong feelings and debate as to what they are and what they signify. The Shroud of Turin is one example. Thought by many to be the actual cloth Jesus was wrapped in after the crucifixion, it is a unique artifact. It shows a *negative* image of a bearded man. Since there was no such thing in the world as a negative image before the invention of photography in the 19th century, it is highly unlikely that anyone in the past could have stumbled on this technique to create a picture or image. I have read that there were pollen grains found on the shroud that could only have come from the area of Palestine. Yet recent carbon dating of the shroud puts its creation squarely in the middle ages. Is it a fake? Yes it is, but that doesn't mean it isn't important. There is a simple explanation for the inconsistencies. The Shroud of Turin is probably a very good copy of a lost original. But why would it be a copy?

The Shroud was probably stolen from Constantinople during the Fourth Crusade in 1204 when the Europeans sacked the city. Constantinople was far more civilized than any city in Europe at that time, which was just beginning to stir itself out of the Dark Ages. The Crusaders themselves, compared to the people of the Hellenistic and Arab world, were a bunch of uneducated and dangerous thugs. The people of Constantinople, having come to know the caliber of what the Europeans were like from their experience with the three previous crusades, would have taken precautions. I suspect that the priests in Constantinople had a good idea what was coming and created an exact copy of the shroud, then hid the original. The real shroud could still be in its hiding place, somewhere within the walls or under the floor of Hagia Sophia in Istanbul.

Archaeologists can only work with what they can find. How objects are found is an important consideration. Recently two *ossuaries* have turned up that have focused attention on New Testament times. Ossuaries are small carved stone boxes used for burying the disarticulated bones of the dead after the flesh has decomposed. The first had the name of Caiaphas on it and could be the actual box containing the bones of the Sadducee judge who condemned Jesus. It was found in a small cave or tomb during the construction of a road project in Jerusalem. The second is called the Jesus Box, because writing on the side says it is the burial box for James, son of Joseph, brother of Jesus. James is mentioned both in the Bible and by the historian Josephus, and was one of the first martyrs. Like the new-found Gospel of Judas, this ossuary came to light through an antiquities dealer and not from a dig, so it was viewed with great suspicion. Some scientists declared it genuine, while others have declared it a fake. This conclusion is based on a single test by a single archaeologist that many other scholars don't accept. The head of antiquities in Israel refuses to let the box be tested again by independent laboratories.[4] The antiquities trader, tried in court for creating the ossuary's inscription, was recently let go, his case dismissed. The government could not prove it was a fake.

The scholarly establishment is dead set against publishing or even acknowledging "unprovenanced" finds which surface through the antiquities market, because they think it encourages looting of historical sites. It is a stand off that engenders debate and much rancor. Scholars will continue to dig and ordinary people living near ancient ruins will continue to sift through ancient garbage, hoping to get lucky. They sell their finds to antiquities dealers and the dealers sell them to eager collectors who want to hold a piece of ancient history. We have two disparate sources of the past and both are needed. But the scholars want all the history to come exclusively through them.

It is exciting to find new pieces of the past from the archaeological digs and other discoveries. I love reading about new finds because it does help make the past seem more real and more a part of the present. But the past will always be the past, and the important work for us is today, in the present. Also, while scientists all over the world view themselves as dispassionate and neutral discoverers of scientific truth, whenever their particular truth is questioned by a fresh discovery or theory, they act just like everybody else when threatened and do all they can to denounce and deny the new evidence. Look at all the major discoveries that have happened in the last hundred years and see how long it has taken the scientific community to change its collective mind. Generally, it takes decades, even despite often overwhelming evidence. Taking sides in any debate, especially the most scholarly, is risky business. The origin of the term, "Big Bang" was actually a put down from a scientist who didn't believe the new theory.

Archaeology is a fascinating subject and finds are always interesting but no new find is ever going to change the meaning of the parables and sayings in the Gospels. Nor will any discovery invalidate the stories Jesus told. The parables mean what they mean. We can choose to believe and practice them, or not. It doesn't matter what any group of people say, be they from a well known university, or any so-called religious authority. We are the ones who ultimately have to make the decision on what we are going to believe and how we are going to behave based on those beliefs.

Render Unto Caesar

The Pharisees came to Jesus and asked him whether or not Jews should pay taxes. In this story, emphasis is put on how the Pharisees were trying to trap Jesus into saying something that would get him in enough trouble so he could be prosecuted or condemned. This was a very cunning question because if he answered either "yes" or "no" he would have been in trouble. Jesus asked for a coin and asked whose face was on the coin. The answer was "Caesar," and Jesus told them, *"Render unto Caesar what is Caesar's, and render unto God what is God's."*

Jesus' response to the question is much more than just a clever answer to an attempted verbal ambush. It is one of the big lessons. Rome collected taxes in order to run the Empire. The disciple Matthew was one of the tax collectors. Caesar was the Emperor of Rome and was considered by most Romans to have god-like stature, even though everyone knew from the first Caesar's example that a few quick knives can make short work of any earthly god. Still, whichever Caesar was in power, he was the embodiment of the Empire.

For the Jews, the question was important. Paying taxes to a foreign power they didn't want or believe in, a power that worked against their own best interests and beliefs, was not only onerous, it went against religious law. Paying taxes directly supported the Roman pagan gods and this violated the Ten Commandments. Today many people get upset when a small part of their tax money is used for programs they don't believe in like stem cell research or funding for stockpiles of weapons. Paying taxes for things that you are opposed to is just as onerous today as it was for the pious in Israel two thousand years ago.

But who is Caesar today? To whom do we render? Our federal government is the first answer that comes to mind. But then, we also have to render to our state governments, our county governments, and to our city governments. As far as taxes go, there are a host of financial obligations we have to deal with daily. Caesar is all this, and more.

The United States is a corporation, which is defined as any group of people seen as united or of one body. Our country is an idea enclosed by lines on a map. The lines don't exist in reality, even along borders where fences follow the invisible lines. Yet we say we are on this side, and others unlike us are on that side. People on either side of the line are real and very much the same. Only the lines are imaginary. They are called *political* maps because the people, the *polis*, decide where they exist and what it means to be on one side or the other.

Jesus paid little attention to nationality or background. The two people who impressed him the most with their faith, the Centurion and the Samaritan woman, were completely outside mainline Jewish society. Jesus also found great value among the worst sinners, the ones "proper" people would shun. People are valuable. Artificial people, that is, corporations, aren't real and therefore don't even exist. God doesn't bless America. God has never blessed America because America isn't real. It is an area of land within which the people have agreed to certain tenets, laws, obligations, and taxes. If you think about all the corporations we belong to you can see how numerous are the demands for our loyalty. Any one of these groups can become an idol if we let it. We all know people who so strongly identify with some group they belong to that if their membership suddenly ended they would be completely lost.

Each group we belong to represents Caesar. Each group has obligations and benefits for members. We pay our taxes and follow the laws; in return the government provides us with protections and regulations that help large numbers of people live in close proximity with a minimum of conflict.

Non-governmental groups are similar and can also be considered Caesar. Political parties and unions fall into this category. If we belong to a club like Rotary or the Chamber of Commerce, there are dues to pay, obligations to perform, and we receive the benefits of a social or business network, and a meal now and then. We render unto Caesar.

Our churches are another corporate group. They have rules and obligations for membership and benefits for their congregations. God doesn't bless churches either, because they have no more a soul or reality than our town or county or the local PTA.

Groups tend to reflect the general thinking of their members. If a group is hijacked by a charismatic or fearful leader, it can be led just about anywhere. When a fearful person who thinks they know who the enemies are and what to do about them gets control of the state during a stressful time, bad things happen. Wars start. Armed forces, the instruments of fear, are enlarged. One of the good things about our three-branch form of government is that it is more difficult to hijack.

One church I knew of had a policy of changing its pastor every two years or so; the rationale was that the congregation needed to pay attention to the message and not the man. The outgoing pastor was as loving and forgiving a person as you could find, while the new one was concerned with adherence to the church's teaching and kept a watchful eye for infractions. The personality of the church changed almost overnight from being an organization that welcomed outsiders to being closed and suspicious and overly concerned with dogma. The message preached from the pulpit was supposed to be the same, but the church came to reflect the fears of the new minister.

No matter what its stated purpose, once a group is formed, it begins to take on a corporate consciousness of its own. Issues and questions arise and need to be addressed. Decisions need to be made. Requirements need to be formulated and responsibilities delegated. No matter how much the members may try to do things differently or how they go about making their decisions, the process used is the same for most groups. Problems that arise between personalities are minimized or accommodated, material needs for the group and for the individual members are brought up and addressed, while plans are made to deal with the common fears each particular group has. Generally, groups end up choosing a middle-of-the-road path that most of the members can follow and support. This is even true of groups on the lunatic fringes, whose members still show a diversity of beliefs. But this is *not* true for groups who follow an authoritive leader who demands that all followers believe exactly as he does. With these groups there is only one point of view and everyone has to parrot the party line.

So what is the rule for dealing with any corporate entity or group? *Render unto Caesar what is Caesar's.*

We can be a member of most any group we want by paying our dues and participating. If we don't want to render, we can drop out. If we don't like the local government, we can move. Sometimes we can fight city hall, sometimes we can't. Governments have provisions for this. If we really don't want to go along with part of our government obligations, we can work to find a way around them. This is usually not easy. Being a pacifist or a conscientious objector during wartime has always been difficult, but it can be done. One of the main reasons people get upset dealing with government is that it seems so soulless, which underscores what we have been discussing. It does no good to get angry at something that doesn't exist. We can only vent on some poor government worker or bureaucrat, who probably doesn't like working for the government all that much either.

Jesus was not a Christian; he was a good Jew. It is not necessary to be a Christian to follow the teachings of Jesus. It is good to remember that of all the people who actually saw Jesus and heard him speak two thousand years ago, not a single one was a Christian. His followers weren't called by that name until long after the Resurrection.

Jesus wasn't concerned with labels. He saw everyone as children of God and all children of God have the same needs. It is true that many of the people he met were involved in activities that contradicted his teachings, but that hasn't changed either. As far as his most important lessons are concerned, we are all in that boat. We think labels of identity are important but they were not important to Jesus.

Groups cannot save or damn us but they can provide an environment that will either increase or decrease our sense of well-being. If being a member of a particular group seems to help you and adds to your sense of peace and happiness, it is good. If membership stops being helpful, begins causing friction or difficulties—if you find you are more fearful than before—then find another group that better fits you and your life. Vote with your feet. If you are feeling poor and think you need more money, stop tithing. Instead of tithing, consider taking some money and actually giving it to people who are in need. After all, Jesus told his followers to give to the poor. He did not tell them to give to organizations who will then give some of what they get to the poor.

If you find yourself in a job or situation where you seem to be surrounded by "enemies", then it could conceivably be the best place for you at the moment, since changing your mind about your "enemies" is a bigger priority than being with people who share your beliefs.

Of course, the most important part of this saying of Jesus is, *"Render unto God what is God's."* The corporate groups we find ourselves in and those we seek out can have much or little meaning to us. We can make of them what we will. We tend to define ourselves by the jobs we have or the groups we belong to. When this happens the group can become a little god, an idol that is almost worshipped. For this reason, some people find that belonging to as few organizations as possible simplifies their lives and makes the work of living easier.

Groups can become ends in themselves, rather than ways to have a better experience in life. One way to decide about joining or staying in any group is to see it as either leading us toward or away from the love of God and appreciation for our brothers and sisters. Despite the stated goals of any group, to find out what it is really like, you need to be a member for a while. We have all been in groups that were begun under one premise but became something totally different.

Usually, the main agenda of any organization is its continued existence and growth. Groups are artificial persons and so they act much like a simple living organism in the Darwinian sense. They want to eat (ask for money) and grow. Most groups want to make some kind of difference in the world. It is important to remember that groups are just social organizations that we give meaning to. They do not give meaning to us.

Then there is also the tendency to want to help lead and have a say in the direction the group is going. No matter what the group, becoming a leader is a perilous proposition. There is a great deal of unforeseen baggage that comes with the position of being a leader. There is always the possibility that you could become a Pharisee.

Pharisees—Then and Now

Jesus talked to the Pharisees often. They seemed to be with him much of the time, and the disciples said they were up to no good. Most of Jesus' references to the Pharisees were negative. Today the word is defined as being a sanctimonious, hypocritical, self-righteous person, but that definition tells us nothing about the ancient Pharisees.

There has also been a change in the way the word is used by modern scholars. They write that the way the ancient Pharisees viewed God, the world and man's relationship to both, have evolved into what today is mainstream Judaism. Some scholars now use the term to mean a system of religious thought, and not one of several separate religious sects of Israel two thousand years ago. Using the term in this way, some scholars state that Jesus himself was also a Pharisee. And this is true, in that his words make it clear he was much closer in his thinking to the Pharisees than he was to the Sadducees.

The problem with this new definition is that the word Pharisee, when used in a negative way as it has historically been used, and as it is used in the New Testament, can now be labeled vaguely anti-Semitic. I am using the term to mean members of the mainline political/religious authority in Israel during the time of Jesus' ministry. No matter what their professed beliefs, almost all men in authority generally react in the same way as the Pharisees did to perceived challenges and threats to their authority and beliefs. I know of no good single word that defines a person in a position of authority in some group who consciously chooses to always protect and further the goals of his organization over what his conscience would dictate. *Pharisee* is a good enough word for this kind of person.

During Jesus' time, the Pharisees were the dominant religious sect in Israel. They shared religious power and authority with the Sadducees, whose beliefs differed somewhat. For example, the Sadducees didn't believe in angels or in the existence of an immortal soul. The Sadducees were even stricter about following the law than the Pharisees. However, the Pharisees were strict enough that the name has come to mean anyone who puts the letter of the law above the spirit. Both Pharisees and Sadducees had a strong sense of self-righteousness and little tolerance for deviation from religious law. It is an observable fact that many people in a position to monitor the behavior of others become self-righteous in doing so. It is a mantle that often goes with the office.

The Essenes were another Jewish sect in the area during the time of Jesus. They were an insular ascetic religious community that believed the Day of Judgment was imminent. *The Dead Sea Scrolls*, found in caves above the Essenes settlement at Qumran, show that Jesus was well aware of the teachings of the Essenes.

Other than the gospels, just about the only written source that covers the history of Israel during New Testament times is Flavius Josephus. Josephus was a Pharisee and even mentions Jesus in one paragraph, although this writing, the first published mention of Jesus, was later "enhanced" by someone in the early Christian church. Josephus was born shortly after Jesus died and was a participant in the Jewish rebellion against

Rome. He was captured and taken to Rome early in the conflict. With the Emperor Vespasian as his patron, he wrote an extensive history of the war and the Jewish people. Following the conventions of writing of his time, he listed his ancestry and education so that he would be accepted as a competent author capable of handling his subject. Josephus claimed he attended the school of the Pharisees, the school of the Sadducees as well as the school of the Essenes. Finally he spent three years in the desert with a mystic wearing skins and eating only wild food, living the same life as did John the Baptist a few decades before.[5]

Josephus claimed this educational experience in order to prove his authority. It would be like someone today citing their degrees from prestigious universities or their experience with certain groups. Since Josephus claimed it, he wouldn't have been the only person to have had this experience. If one was to write about what it was to be Jewish and about their practice of religion, it would be a great benefit to have experienced each of the major areas of faith. The ancient world was curious about the Jews because Jewish practices were so different. They were considered to be a deeply philosophical people because they only worshipped one God. But they were viewed with suspicion because they never partook of the religious celebrations of the Empire and set themselves apart with their dietary restrictions and the practice of circumcision.

Josephus wrote his books in Rome after Jerusalem had been destroyed and had no worries that someone would check his resume. The fact that Josephus felt the need to claim such an extensive religious background means that this is what an exceptional Jew, one who wanted to understand the entire religious experience of being Jewish, would do. He also claimed to have been a prodigy in his youth, with important people seeking him out for his advice when he was just fourteen. Does this sound familiar?

I think it is a reasonable assumption that Josephus claimed the experience that Jesus actually had. That in fact, Jesus set the precedent for someone who knew and could speak about all the different groups in Israel.

The Pharisees would not have defined themselves as hypocritical. The term hypocrite means someone who professes beliefs he does not really hold—a phony. The Pharisees saw themselves as simply acting in the best interests of the law as they understood it. Their beliefs were strong and they tried to live their beliefs as best they could. They had a reputation for piety and many had no love of luxury. The Pharisees worked hard studying the law. As religious leaders, they were highly respected by the general population.

The authorities in Jerusalem would have heard about this man with a new teaching who seemed to be doing inexplicable things and gathering followers. For them, it was a difficult situation. John the Baptist had been locked up and then killed for pointing out that the ruler of Judea, Herod Antipas, was living in sin. John had many followers and they weren't happy. Now Jesus appears with even more followers. Who knew what would come from this? The Romans were difficult to deal with and dangerous. They didn't care much about the religious beliefs of their subject peoples, but they were very concerned with collecting taxes and keeping order, and there was ongoing and increasing trouble from the Zealots.

The Pharisees in Jerusalem acted the way any authority would act, given the same circumstances. Some of Jesus' teachings seemed to be inspired, while some of them seemed to flout authority and strike at the very heart of Mosaic Law. Some Pharisees began to watch him and ask him questions, seeking to lead him into breaking the law or committing blasphemy, which is slander against God. Blasphemy was considered high treason, a crime punishable by death. It is still considered so in the Islamic world, where any criticism or unholy depiction of Allah or the Prophet is met with outrage and retribution. If you would like to know what daily life was like in the time of Jesus, living in a conservative Islamic country is probably as close as you can get in the world today. This is not a condemnation. Jesus appeared and taught in a very conservative, very religious country and spoke a universal message of freedom that could be practiced within the religious and cultural restrictions of his time. If what he said applied in that situation, then we should have fewer problems applying his teachings in our own land and time.

The Pharisees were only being prudent and cautious, traits which are considered worthy in leaders. They didn't see in Jesus what the common people did. They didn't look at him with their hearts, but only with their heads. Even this is a little surprising, given that there was a lot of expectation that the Messiah would come soon and the Pharisees knew scripture better than anyone else. They knew the events that the prophets had foretold, and also something about what the nature of the Messiah should be. Yet, when he was among them, almost all the Pharisees failed to see him as the fulfillment of prophecy and rejected him. This calls into question the emphasis many churches today put on studying the Bible and believing in it as literal truth. The Pharisees did just that and as a group, completely failed to understand what the prophesies foretold. Even after two thousand years, there is still little understanding of the basic principles that Jesus taught. Dostoyevsky noted this in his story, *The Grand Inquisitor.* The Grand Inquisitor for the Spanish Inquisition actually tries Jesus as a heretic and condemns him—for the good of the Church.

The Pharisees didn't recognize Jesus for who he was for several reasons. One is that most people assumed that the expected Messiah would be an earthly leader who would free Israel from Roman rule. This turned out not to be the case. The Messiah obviously did not come to make things better on earth. It has been two thousand years, and not much is better. We have a tendency to think that technological progress has greatly improved our lives, but this really isn't the case. We can travel much faster and farther, but this isn't a change for the better either. It's just a change. The big improvement everyone points to is in medicine, because we have drastically decreased infant mortality by eliminating many childhood diseases. But in the past, a larger percentage of the population reached and exceeded the age of one hundred. Most of the positive changes we have today are due to improvements in public health. Drinking pure water and pasteurized milk and having our wastes go into sewers ended many of the common deadly diseases. However, disease itself is on the rise again.

Nowadays many people spend the second half of their lives with chronic illnesses. We live under the new threat of much more virulent diseases as well. Because of improvements in transportation and our faster lifestyle, a "super bug" can travel to every corner of the world in a matter of weeks.

Our standard of living is extremely high compared to how people lived in the ancient world. Most people in the industrialized nations today live as well as only the highest classes of two thousand years ago. In many ways, we are better off than the kings and queens of old. We are so well off, we have to create exotic diversions for ourselves in order not to become bored.

We have enough to eat, we think we have a good chance of handling most of the common diseases, and we don't fear armed invasion from abroad. We have what has always been seen as a "good life," and the way we live would be envied by almost everyone in history. We should be happy and feel secure, but we aren't and we don't.

We seem to have a need to be afraid. If one fear is suddenly extinguished, another immediately takes its place. Starting just after World War II and continuing for almost fifty years we lived under the dire threat of nuclear annihilation. The Doomsday Clock was set for only a few minutes before midnight, when a nuclear war would begin and much of the life on earth would be wiped out. Then the Cold War ended. It was suddenly over, the competition between superpowers was gone. We should have all breathed a great sigh of relief, but with hardly a pause from one to the other, new fears—global warming, climate change and the threat of terrorism—took the place of the old.

One measure of success for any society is the level of fear—or its complement, how safe and secure people feel about their lives. Using this measure, nothing has changed in two thousand years.

There are a few things that at first appear to be better. Today, when this or that group or government practices genocide, they generally try to hide it and when caught, they deny it. Claiming the Holocaust never happened is an example. In the old days, getting rid of a group of people who were seen as evil or not in

God's favor was considered a religious duty. This is where the term Holy War came from. It is a war that God sanctioned in order to rid the earth of some group of unholy or unworthy people. Almost everyone today at least pays lip service to the idea that wholesale slaughter is wrong and that we are, in truth, one people. Yet there is no appreciable reduction of genocide. In the last hundred years we have become very skilled at killing large numbers of people quickly and efficiently.

Another reason so many didn't see Jesus as the Messiah was that his simple message of love and forgiveness was at odds with the problems of living in a land occupied by a foreign power. In a climate of fear and blame, it is very difficult to give up your fears and see the very ones you blame as your brothers. The idea of intentionally giving up conflict, the outgrowth of fear and blame, is truly revolutionary and very hard to accept. This is why Jesus called the Pharisees hypocrites. They were using the law not to know God better, but to condemn a perceived threat. They ignored any evidence that went counter to their perceptions—as Jesus went from a "person of interest" to a substantial threat, he triggered all of the alarms and set in motion all of the events that would lead to his capture, trial and death on the cross. Even today, to truly follow Jesus means giving up almost all the ideas we take for granted about justice, fairness, judgment and fear.

Despite the nativity story told in the gospels, it is obvious that by the time of Jesus' ministry, word of a special child having been born according to prophesy had not become generally known. Jesus made small waves when he stayed at the Temple in Jerusalem when he was 12, speaking with wisdom to the elders in the Temple, but this did not help him twenty years later. Jesus was reviled in his own town of Nazareth by his own neighbors when he announced the beginning of his ministry, so there was clearly no expectation on the part of the authorities or those who knew him that he was marked for anything special.

The people who accepted him did so because of who he appeared to be and the message he taught, not because he had a great pedigree. With one or two exceptions, the Pharisees didn't accept him at all.

We make the mistake of the Pharisee when we are so locked into our vision of the world with all its fears and small rewards that we are unable to see or act outside of it. We have determined what the problems are and the acceptable and unacceptable solutions available. The world now conforms to our judgments and we are closed to outside, or contrary points of view. We also confuse our own interests and prejudices with those of our group, nation, or even all of mankind.

The Pharisee thinks he knows the mind of God and what is contrary to it. He does all he can to further God's interests and impede anything that seems to oppose them. All of this is done in the name of God for the good of all believers. The Pharisee is locked into a mindset that requires constant judgment and makes forgiveness difficult.

So who are the Pharisees of today and how can we avoid becoming one?

Any leader can act like a Pharisee when he confuses the good of the organization with the greater good of humankind. In religious circles, Pharisees are members in some position of authority. They can be ministers, rabbis, pastors, priests, members of a church board, managers, deacons, teachers, secretaries, or hold any other position with the opportunity to make or change policy of the organization or monitor the behavior of members. They are respected for their positions and have a stake in the status quo. This last part is very important. People work hard for money, but we have all seen that people work even harder for position and power. In most religious organizations, the monetary returns are small or non-existent. It is not surprising that in those religious organizations that do bring in a lot of money, almost any change or question is seen as a threat to the organization. The money almost always becomes more important than the message. In some successful churches, so much time and emphasis is put on contributions and fund raising it is obvious that the money *is* the message.

In the ancient world, religion was a business too. In the New Testament there is one story about a problem Paul had that rings very true. In the city of Ephesus, there were artisans who crafted and sold silver images of Artemis of Ephesus, the goddess of the hunt, the huntress who resided in the Temple of Ephesus, one of the Seven Wonders of the World. These craftsmen were afraid the converts to the new teaching of Jesus would put them out of business. They wanted the authorities to make the disciples leave the city and Paul was even imprisoned there for a time. It is a pity none of the early followers of Jesus had the foreknowledge to tell these craftsmen not to worry, all they had to do was start making silver fish and crucifixes to sell to the new believers.

The history of Christianity from the time the Church first became the official religion of the Roman Empire is a history of resistance to change. Once established, a bureaucracy becomes self-perpetuating. The Church fought most advances in science, democracy, and other political and social movements. The efforts from within to align the Church more closely with Jesus' teachings were either stopped or viewed with great suspicion.

Those who were outspoken in their desire for change were labeled heretics and were either forced to recant or were killed.

When Martin Luther broke with the Church in 1517 and started the Protestant Reformation, he questioned the whole foundation of the Church. The Church reacted the way any threatened organization would. It did its best to get hold of Luther so he could be silenced, but when that failed, those in power in the church tried to minimize his teachings. Luther's reformation succeeded because he was protected by the local royalty. They immediately saw the benefits that a ten percent tithe formerly going to Rome would bring to their kingdoms. (Germany became a patchwork quilt of separate Protestant and Catholic kingdoms. The people had to practice the religion of their local prince. This is the real reason why Germany didn't become a unified nation or a power in the world until after 1881.)

Luther quickly built an organization that would, in a few short years, act just as imperiously as the church he left. Luther saw the Pharisees for who they were, and then became one himself. Unfortunately, this pattern happens all too often.

It is very difficult to be in a position of authority, especially at or near the top of an organization, and not become a Pharisee. Being a leader cements a person into a position where following a path in the world becomes the highest priority. Because of this, actually trying to follow what Jesus said is extremely difficult. The leader is locked into his organization's view of the world. Its gains are his gains, its losses his defeats.

Individuals with a large number of followers who are famous for having a single point of view on one or many issues are also locked into that mindset. If they change their minds it is a betrayal of their followers. Still, Jesus told us that the most important thing is to change our minds.

It is good to remember that Jesus never asked for leaders, only followers. We can't be leaders on the road back to God. Remember what he said about being in first place:

"Whoever wants to be the most important person must take the last place and be a servant to everyone else."

This is one of the most difficult lessons because it runs so contrary to conventional wisdom, which holds that personal power is like money, more is always better. Don't strive to become a leader and don't cherish the perks of office. (To become a leader usually means becoming a Pharisee.) It is the polar opposite of being meek and one of the most common traps of the world. The problem of the Pharisee is blindness to the teachings of love, peace, and forgiveness, forsaking them for short-term recognition and worldly gain. Leadership always seems to elevate the person above his peers, and that is probably why it is dangerous for us. It makes it much harder for us to see each other as equals.

Judas, Caiaphas, Pontius Pilate

The recent discovery and publication of the *Gnostic Gospel of Judas* has caused many to rethink the traditional story of Jesus' betrayal. Scholars think this gospel first appeared about a hundred years after Judas died. It is one of the Gnostic gospels, like the others discovered in the *Nag Hamadi* cache in Egypt in the late 1940s that were translated and published in the 1970s.

The Gospel of Judas portrays the betrayal as a plan known to both Judas and Jesus. Many Gnostic beliefs were quite strange and declared heretical early in the history of the Christian movement. One Gnostic interpretation involved both a true God, and a lesser "god of the world" which explained why things were so bad in the world. The Gnostic picture of God and the world probably came through the early Greek and Roman followers of Jesus, who tried to make sense of his message within their own context of belief which involved many gods and secret teachings. Judas was one who was supposed to have received some of the secrets from Jesus.

It is important to see Judas' role differently from that of the traditional evil betrayer of Jesus. Anyone who gives any thought to the betrayal in light of what Jesus said cannot really come to any other conclusion.

Obviously, if Jesus preached love for one's enemies, then he must have loved those who didn't agree with him or who saw him as a threat to scripture and to the stability of the state of Israel. It is clear from the words of the disciples that a number of people considered Jesus to be an enemy. But if Jesus didn't love those who saw him as dangerous, then there would not be much point in following him because he would have been a hypocrite himself.

Jesus loved those who considered themselves his enemies, and they included the Romans, Judas, and the Pharisees. Jesus himself would have seen nobody as an enemy. He was just in contact with many people who didn't understand him or his message. He forgave them because they didn't know what they were doing. We can assume from the other things he said that he didn't condemn them for this. Any condemnation we read into scripture is probably from the disciples, who had just as hard a time with judgment and forgiveness as we do today and who were understandably upset and angry over what had been done to Jesus.

We can also assert that if Jesus was who he said he was, he would know exactly what was going to happen to him. The betrayal by Judas could not have come as a surprise and so there would not have been any condemnation of Judas when it happened.

Jesus' birth and death followed the ancient prophesies. It really doesn't make much sense to us today, because we are so far removed from the world of two thousand years ago. The prophesies that foretold the coming of the Messiah were made in the context of the ancient world. At that time, there were hundreds of gods, all of whom demanded sacrifice. Some demanded human sacrifice. One of the reasons the family-centered Romans so hated the Carthaginians was that the Phoenician gods demanded a supreme sacrifice. Whenever a serious threat against Carthage loomed, the temple priests told the people sacrifices were required. The Carthaginians, including even the rulers, brought their own children to the temples and threw them alive into red-hot iron ovens made in the likeness of their god.

In the old days, Yahweh too demanded sacrifice. Thinking that he had been told to sacrifice his son, Abraham got the knife and was ready to do the deed. If God told you to do it, you had to do it. It is clear from this story, that some time back in the centuries before Abraham, God didn't tell them to stop when the knife was held high. Today when someone says that God told them to kill their children we put them away in a mental institution. Almost nobody believes that God could ask this of us. The Father that Jesus described in his parables and teachings would never do this. Not then, not now, not ever.

However, Jesus' role in the forgiveness of sin is still put into the context of ancient sacrifice. There is widespread belief that sacrifice is necessary; but this in itself augments fear. God asked Abraham to sacrifice his son, and then relented. But much later, we are asked to accept that God sacrifices his own Son for the good of the world. It is difficult to love or trust a God who would allow the killing of his own son. Jesus asked us repeatedly to see God as our loving father and to see ourselves as his beloved children. Remember, another lesson of the crucifixion is that even the most horrible death doesn't cause lasting injury.

The only way to get right with God in the old days was sacrifice. That is what all the temples in the ancient world were for. They were the places where sacrificial offerings and gifts for the gods were placed on altars to gain favor and avoid their anger.

In order for Jesus' life to follow the prophesies, everything had to happen just the way it did. His birth had to follow the prophesies of his birth, and his death had to do the same. Two thousand years ago his life was in the context of sacrifice because that was part of the universal culture. Judas had to turn Jesus over to the authorities; Caiaphas, the Sadducee judge, had to find Jesus guilty and turn him over to the Romans; Pontius Pilate had to find him guilty and have him crucified. Each person had to play his part or the prophesies would not have been fulfilled. Each person *did* play his role, hard as it was. Without their contributions, Jesus' ministry would not have followed the scriptures.

Just as it is today, ritual and tradition were important to the people of the ancient world. Everything they did had an order to it that was passed down from their fathers and grandfathers. The people needed to know that their belief had a scriptural basis. It helped their faith, even though it was never necessary to sacrifice animals or even to go to the Temple to be closer to God. But we are much like them, and even today it makes most of us feel better to go to a special place that is somewhat set apart from the world.

The peoples of the ancient world created priesthoods to do the rituals and ceremonies to seek the gods' favors. These practices were done in holy places and temples. The priesthood would make up the rules, and tell the people what their obligations were. Priests were considered to be special people, closer to the gods because of their position. They are still often thought of as such, even though worldly evidence shows they are no different than the rest of us. The priesthood would always ask for sacrifice, because they have always had a keen eye for any behavior that goes against the communal norms. The priesthood would also share in some of the peoples' obligatory gifts, which means that they had to keep asking for tithes, and reminding the people to remember their obligations.

It is difficult for us to imagine forgiving a Judas. It was just as difficult for the disciples, so we are in good company. They weren't very good at following Jesus' teachings either. Throughout the New Testament, there is a continuing refrain of blame towards those who did not accept Jesus and the new teachings or those who tried to impede or stop the disciples' work. In some of these instances, God was supposed to have had these people killed for their unbelief. According to Jesus, God is love, and therefore he doesn't go around whacking people who don't have the right beliefs or who haven't yet changed their minds. But the message that God punishes those who don't believe correctly has come down intact through the centuries. The complementary belief, that God rewards those who are righteous with worldly gifts— despite all that Jesus said about worldly things— is also alive and claimed by many.

There is a very simple truth here. God does not punish. He could not do so and still be a good shepherd. We are the ones who call for punishment and then ask God to finish the action of our own judgment. One of my high school friends had a German belt buckle from WWI. It was solid brass and stamped, *Gott Mit Uns*, which means, "God with us," or more loosely, "God is on our side." This was a military belt buckle so the implicit message is that God is *not* on the side of our enemies. Many Germans still thought this way in WWII. However, it is a true statement, and true for everyone, always, because there is, in truth, only one side to be on no matter what is going on in the world.

Jesus reaffirmed to us that God is love. I think that it might be useful to compare our image of God with the image of a good human father. We know what a good father should do. He should love his children and keep them from harm. Jesus addressed this very situation directly when he said:

"If your child asks you for bread, would any of you give him a stone? If you then, imperfect as you are, know how to give to your children, how much more will your Father in Heaven give to those who ask Him?"

If we think God is capable of doing anything to any of his children that would land a normal father in jail, then our picture of God is probably faulty. For example, throwing millions of his own children into the fires of hell to burn forever would make God worse than any tyrant of history.

Jesus told the disciples that there was much they would learn later. It is clear from the gospel accounts that they weren't fast learners, which should be a comfort to us because we aren't very fast learners either.

You Can't Get There from Here

There is an old joke about a person lost in Maine, who asks a man standing beside the road how to get to a certain town. The local man tells him to go another three miles along the road till he comes to a crossroad and then turn left, then he corrects himself and says he has to turn right, then he corrects himself again telling the stranger to go back the way he came for two miles, then he admits that won't work either and reluctantly tells the stranger, "Come to think of it, you can't get there from here!"

We often choose what we are going to do with our lives based on assumptions that our choices will take us where we want to go, and make our life more meaningful and rewarding in the process. There are underlying assumptions to our decision making. Some are based on hope, and others on fear.

Here is an example. There are more restaurants in this country than any other business, and restaurants also have the largest number of business failures. It is one of the hardest, lowest paying, and most time-consuming professions, yet many people want to open and run a restaurant. We can only understand this desire when we acknowledge a deep felt need to give—to feed people. It is a spiritual need that impels many to open a restaurant and serve others.

Some people decide to become doctors because they fear death. They choose a profession through which they can fight their adversary. Some become psychologists and psychiatrists to better understand themselves and others. And many join the ministry because they think it is how they can be closer to God.

I think many potential pastors and priests have pictures in their minds of a deeply spiritual life like that of the Christian saints of the past. But the reality of a minister's life is much more like a person running a small business. A pastor has a physical plant to manage, a weekly product to deliver, customers who need to be served, and often an overseeing board of directors or lay church members that have input on every decision. The small problems, concerns, and duties are far removed from the dream of a contemplative spiritual life.

There are problems with most worldly dreams. Take the great desire to become a pilot, a dream I share. The dream of flying is to soar freely as a bird, to let go of the confines of gravity. But the reality of flight is that, outside of nuclear power plants, there is hardly another human activity so tightly regulated and controlled. Pilots who love to fly put up with the regulations and many actually find freedom within the rules, which is a very good lesson if you think about it. Anyone who can feel a sense of freedom within extreme restrictions is in a good position for life and is already incorporating some of Jesus' teachings. But for most, the dreams of freedom in this world always fall short of expectations.

The truth is, there is no profession that brings us closer to God. We think that some professions are better and more spiritual than others, but real spiritual work can only be done in the mind. It would seem, based on what Jesus said about turning the other cheek, that being in the military would work against following him, and yet the Roman Centurion was his model for faith. So we probably don't need to change our profession. But we do need to change our minds about how we do it.

When individuals have a spiritual breakthrough, they often feel the need to follow this with a profound change in their lives. They think they need to do something more spiritual than whatever they were doing before. Those who feel this way often fail at their new endeavor, which is very confusing. First, they think God blessed them, but then God doesn't bless their new spiritual effort to get closer to Him. If there is any lesson in this, it would be that it is probably not a good idea to make your living from your spiritual work. We are told not to lend money to friends, and there is a good reason for this. It can lower the friendship to the level of the loan, cheapening the relationship. If the money isn't paid back the friendship is at risk. How much more important then, is our spiritual work?

Put quite simply, if you are making a living from your spiritual work, you probably don't have much of a spiritual life. You have a business, a job, a profession. A business can masquerade as spiritual activity for a long time, especially if it is successful. There is still a generalized belief that if someone is successful in the world, God is showing favor. But being successful at any endeavor in the world doesn't translate into spiritual advancement, although the opposite is sometimes true. There are many stories of people seeing the light after they have totally failed or suffered greatly in some other way. It is obvious that in most human activities, failure is a better teacher than success. But there are different kinds of success, and there are different kinds of learning.

One kind of learning is of the world, with which we are all familiar. It is the learning that comes through education and experience. This learning is what we have absorbed from all the schools we have attended, the classes we have taken, all the books we have read, all the people we have met, and all the other experiences large and small that have made an impact on us.

If we want to increase our income or make a significant, planned change in our life, we enroll in classes, buy some books, or apprentice ourselves in some trade or to some mentor and begin the process of building new expertise and experience. It can be tedious and lengthy, but this is how to do it. Honor is given to people with the highest academic degrees because of their learning accomplishment. Many of them do well financially, although a direct correlation between success and education depends less on the amount of education and more on what field they decided to study. Medical doctors usually do well, while doctors of philosophy make far less.

I grew up in Iowa in a university town. My father was an English professor. He told me something that was a well-known piece of advice given to university presidents. "Be kind to your A students, because they will go out and make discoveries and write books and reflect well on your school. And be kind to your B students, because they will go out and get good jobs and have children and send them to your university when they are of age. But be especially kind to your C students, because some of them will go out and make millions of dollars and then they will give you some."

This turned out to be true for Iowa State. An ISU graduate named C. Y. Stevens was only a C student but loved his time in Ames. He made a lot of money and gave ISU a million dollars to start construction of a new auditorium with his name on it. It is a remarkable building, looking a bit like a nun's hat, and has perfect acoustics. ISU was so proud of it they brought in the New York Philharmonic to perform the inaugural concert.

The man who started Federal Express got the idea for it while he was in college. He put it into a paper for a business class and got a C on the paper. The professor couldn't see the vision.

Degrees don't necessarily translate into more money. More importantly, they don't help a person become kinder. University faculty meetings are often filled with an amazing amount of disagreement and rancor. University people do tend to have better vocabularies, so the put downs are sometimes more sophisticated, but they are still attacks. Plato thought that the most enlightened rule for society would be a government of "philosopher kings." From what I have seen of our present day philosophers, this would be a grave mistake.

You can't learn anything important about either God or Jesus in a university. Universities can only teach what is already generally known and as I have previously said, every copy of the New Testament contains just about all the source material there is on Jesus. At universities, when there is a lack of universal agreement on any subject, the divergent views are expressed and discussed. This means that intensive scholarship on the New Testament only shows how little agreement there is on what actually happened. Church supported universities usually present only their own religion's accepted teaching and discourage all others.

We have seen that highly educated people tend to make as many mistakes as anybody else. Most important life-changing lessons are learned through direct experience rather than from education. And sometimes our experience can take us into strange territories indeed, where our previous education is of no help at all.

But there is another kind of knowledge and another kind of learning. The results for this other kind of learning are far less dependable than a university education, but are much more striking. It is the kind of learning the disciples gained after the Resurrection. It changed them from cringing criminal associates to men of faith, unafraid to speak to anyone and everyone of a new and different way of life. This is the learning spoken of by mystics of all religions. It is what waits at the end of long meditations. It can come suddenly on a street corner in Louisville, Kentucky, as it did to a young Father Merton, just out of his cloister for the first time in months, when he realized that everyone he saw was a beloved child of God.

This knowledge is sometimes called being born again or having an epiphany or becoming enlightened. There are other terms. The Quakers say it is a *leading* or an *opening*. Sometimes it is called revelation, but that term is a little too strong for me. I have never had a revelation but I have had moments that were not of this world and so have many of the people I know. This second kind of learning is about oneness, peace, and love, experienced by many as told in books and testimony. There are moments that defy description yet leave us fundamentally changed. If this happens, you suddenly realize there are no questions. There is just peace and complete understanding. The descriptions of these moments are all inadequate. Those who have had the experience are clearly frustrated by their inability to find the words to explain what happened to them or how important it was. It is obvious from their experiences that the Word of God has almost nothing to do with *words* at all.

The experience comes, then, just as suddenly it is gone, leaving behind only the memory of certainty. My sister, back in the late 1960s, was lying sick in bed with a fever. She was worried about the war in Viet Nam and prayed for understanding. She asked how there could be such a terrible thing as war. In response, she was shown shifting shapes of changing color. The answer was long and complicated, but complete; it made perfect sense, and she understood.

"God speaks in moving blocks of color, you know," she told me later. She has no idea how to articulate the answer she received. But even today, just the memory carries a sense of peace to her. Some people's lives are changed forever. Others, when they think their lives haven't really changed and the feelings aren't repeated, seem to forget the special moment and sink back into the world.

There are two separate kinds of learning, and one does not lead to the other. One is of the world; the other is something else entirely. Intense study will not lead to the second kind of learning. Unlike the learning of the world, there is no dependable, systematic effort that can guarantee results, although those who meditate and spend long periods in prayer seem to have the experience more often. A spiritual practice does help put us in the way of these events, according to some, although it also seems to happen regularly to ordinary people who are not doing anything special.

If there is a common element it has to do with letting go of our fears and worries and stepping away from all the plans we make as we live our normal lives. If we make some space for wonder in our life, and give some time to those things that are not of the world, we probably have a better chance of having these experiences. The common threads are love and kindness, peace, and centering ourselves in the moment. The things that seem to work against it are fear, planning, preoccupation with all the worries of the world, and anger. One of the directions Jesus gave that hardly anyone follows was, *"Do not think about tomorrow."* In other words, if we follow the teachings of Jesus and let go of worldly concerns, we bring ourselves much closer to having this kind of experience. And there is another possible benefit from having this experience. It could be that it is the actual way to find the pearl of great price Jesus spoke of.

It's Not What We Do, It's What We Think

What is faith? Most people think they have it, or at least a degree of it. Jesus said that even a tiny amount of faith, equivalent to a mustard seed, could move mountains. But that kind of faith seems to be beyond belief in this day and age. We know where all the mountains are, and none of them have moved. But we can get closer to the kind of faith Jesus spoke of by examining the best example of faith in the New Testament, the Centurion who asked Jesus to heal his servant. Jesus said he had not seen faith like the Centurion's in all of Israel. The Centurion is a good example of someone who has the kind of faith we all could wish we had. He was an average, competent, military man with a responsible job, so emulating him shouldn't be that much of a stretch. The Centurion had more faith than all the disciples. What was that faith composed of?

He had the absolute conviction that what Jesus said, would happen—with no thoughts to the contrary. The Centurion had no doubts, and his belief was not hobbled by thinking that the laws of the world are fixed. Miracles are, by definition, things that undo the way the world usually works. It follows that a strong belief in the laws of the world must make the occurrence of a miracle more difficult. Our fears, along with our normal everyday thinking, block faith.

Miracles were an essential part of Jesus' ministry. The disciples continued to heal people after the Resurrection. It is clear from reading the contemporary books about Jesus that many scholars don't believe in miracles at all. The belief that miracles are all fabrications isn't new. Thomas Jefferson, a founding father of our country and author of the *Declaration of Independence,* was one of the Deists I mentioned earlier. He created his own translation of the gospels, leaving out every miracle and the Resurrection.

Miracles are incompatible with science. For one thing, miracles can't be studied because they can't be repeated. Most of the evidence for miracles is anecdotal and science doesn't like anecdotal evidence. Science depends on things that other scientists can replicate by following a procedure or recipe. Stories of miracles are either disparaged or ignored. They may be embarrassing to science, but they do exist. Ask almost any group of people how many have personally experienced a miracle and see the hands go up. I am defining a miracle as an event or happening that clearly contradicts the normal scientific laws that the world seems to obey. I am not including the stories of amazing rescues or anything else that can be described as lucky.

There are also thousands of miracles recounted in literature. It is hard to ignore this immense body of experience, but many do, probably because admitting to the possibility of miracles opens the door to things that many people don't want to consider. The study of science tells us how the natural world works and what part we have in it. Miracles undo the thin security of this knowledge and open everything to question.

Miracles happen. It takes an almost superhuman effort to ignore them and try to recreate the story of Jesus' teachings based only on what he said. I don't think the story of Jesus and the advent of Christianity makes any sense without the miracles. Who in their right mind would have followed a man who told them to love their enemies and associate with disreputable people, along with a number of other completely counter-intuitive teachings, unless there was overwhelming evidence that his teachings actually worked?

In my experience, the reason why his ideas are still so powerful is that when you put them into practice you begin to experience your own miracles. And once you have personally experienced a miracle, it becomes the measure of everything else. Miracles trump what we usually call reality. The conundrum is easily stated. If you are a skeptic and have never experienced or believed in the possibility of a miracle, then no explanation of God or Jesus is good enough. If you have experienced one, no explanation is necessary. There is not, nor will there ever be, a scientific explanation of miracles because miracles undo science, along with just about everything else.

When a miracle is experienced, all questions about whether miracles are real or not evaporate. The miracle is real, and may well be the only thing that is. Everything else can be questioned, but not the miracle.

Jesus walked on water. He defied gravity, the most accepted natural law. But remember that Peter also walked on water for a short time, until he came to his senses and nearly drowned. This is what literally happened; our senses tell us when we are in danger. For just an instant, Peter listened to that part of his mind that told him people can't walk on water, and that was enough to undo his faith in Jesus and for gravity to take hold of him again. There are many examples of people and objects defying the law of gravity in a similar way up to the present time. "Little Donkey," Joseph of Cupertino, the patron saint of pilots, spent a good deal of time floating around in the air and out of his senses. According to what is written of him, he was probably mentally challenged, so it may have been easier for him to ignore the laws of the world, not having learned them in the first place.

Can the mind levitate matter? Science says, yes. At least it was yes when I took my Abnormal Psychology class back in college. My textbook mentioned the Poltergeist Phenomena and described it as repeated small events, usually mechanical breakdowns, but there were a few rare instances of bottles and other things flying through the air. Of course, in movies they always start with things flying around. Science has no idea what is happening here, but they do know how to stop it. They just look around the immediate environment for a teenager, almost always a boy, and take him away and give him counseling. As soon as they do that, all the weird stuff stops. The boy, of course, has no idea he was causing the problems and cannot consciously repeat what he caused. But it had to come from some part of his mind.

What goes on in our minds, how we think, and what we think about, is very important. Jesus said that our thinking is more important than anything else. *"It isn't what goes into our mouths that makes us unclean, it is what comes out of our mouths."* The religious authorities had been saying just the opposite about cleanliness and uncleanliness for centuries. All good Jews were careful about what they ate so that they would not become unclean. The disciples were probably very confused about this part of Jesus' message. But the teaching would become even more confusing.

Let's consider the process of thinking for a moment. Before we speak, we create the thoughts in our minds. We know people who have the reputation of speaking before they think, but this isn't what happens. Those people do think before they speak, they just don't go to the trouble of considering the effect of their thoughts on others before they let them out. They don't consider the possible consequences of what they are about to say. We call it shooting from the hip, letting the gun go off as it clears the holster, without pausing to aim. Sometimes there is a certain admiration for this because it shows fearlessness, but we know what usually happens to these people. Eventually they say something that offends someone, and then they suffer the consequences. We are cautioned to be careful of what we say in social and business settings. Good advice—or is it?

Being polite, gracious, politically correct, and prudent, means learning to *not* say what we are really thinking. But the underlying antisocial thoughts are still there.

What comes out of our mouths is often a mistake, but so too are the unspoken thoughts that remain in our minds, according to Jesus. He pointed out one situation that makes everyone uncomfortable.

Jesus said, *"He who has lusted in his heart has already committed adultery."*

This is a very difficult concept to understand, since everyone has done it to some degree. The attributes wished for in another don't necessarily have to be sexual. The wish is for a different, more loving or secure or more exciting experience with someone new and everyone does this. It is what sells romance and adventure books, movies and TV programs.

To go from perceiving sin as a transgression against the law of God to seeing it as merely a random thought is a huge mental leap. On a personal level, we want to believe our thoughts are private, that they don't affect others. We are not in the habit of policing our thoughts. We think they are largely random and harmless. We also want to believe that our thoughts, even those that are mean and small, are innocent and only cause damage if we act on them.

However, everything we do starts as a thought. We know that some of our thoughts are aberrant and should never be acted upon. We know we need to control ourselves when we are angry or when we feel desires that run contrary to law and custom. A staple of the daily news is stories of people who don't stop themselves from acting out whatever thought crosses their minds. But what harm is caused by our thoughts when they aren't acted on?

The main problem is that some thoughts insidiously undermine faith, as Peter learned in his dunking. If you observe your thoughts, and actually write them down, you will find that you have dozens of fear and doubt thoughts every hour. Many of the thoughts we think are normal are also fearful thoughts cloaked in something we think is positive. Thoughts of excitement have a fearful component. This is recognized in the old Chinese curse, "May you live in exciting times." Excitement is the desire to change a situation to something less boring or typical. A roller coaster ride is exciting because it gives an impressive illusion of danger. We entertain ourselves with exciting things and it is natural to think that if our lives were more exciting we would be happier. This attitude makes seeing excitement as a form of fear difficult. Fear of any kind undoes faith and affirms its opposite. If we are to follow the teachings of Jesus, we have to learn to control the part of our mind that wants us to stay in a state of fear, doubt or excitement. We need to begin recognizing our fear thoughts when we are thinking them and then ask ourselves if this is what we really want or is this the way we want to see ourselves. If we want to change our lives, we have to start by changing our mind, the only place where change can begin.

Our minds are much more powerful than we give them credit for, and probably every thought we think is important. Can changing our thoughts really change the world we experience? Is there another world?

Jesus is Coming?

Jesus spoke often about the Kingdom of God being *imminent.* The disciples believed that he would return to them during their lifetimes. There was a sense of immediacy in their evangelism. They believed the time before the dawning of the Kingdom was short. Yet almost two thousand years have passed. Few can stretch faith enough to make *imminent* cover such a long period of time.

After the disciples and the people who had personally known them had all died, this part of Jesus' teaching lost its sense of urgency. There was a flurry of excitement around the turn of the first millennium, when the calendar showed a thousand years had passed since his birth.

Some see the Second Coming as imminent today, and read into worldly events what they think the prophesies in the *Book of Revelations* foretell. Of course, every prediction, explanation, and timetable for the end times has been wrong so far. Some scholars dismiss Jesus' ministry completely because of this seeming contradiction between what he said was coming soon, and what actually happened. So what is the problem here?

Obviously, we have been wrong about when and where the Kingdom of God is or will be, just as we have been wrong about most of Jesus' teachings when we try to apply them to the world we live in. Misinterpretation is another aspect of human nature everybody shares. We misinterpret a lot of things, and what we think would bring us happiness or would complete us are prime examples.

Most of us have had an experience of intense suffering over a perceived loss, only to find out later that the loss would have been worse if we had gotten our own way. Examples are the desire to excel at a sport or activity or the kind of intense love we fall into when we are teens. We decide how the world should be, what needs to happen and how we should be treated, then feel terrible when the world stubbornly refuses to go along with the picture we have created. When we have our minds made up about something we think we really need—for example the sometimes extreme behavior and fallout stemming from a "mid-life crisis"—no authority in the world can dissuade us from what we are sure we must have. We can even drop friends and family on our quest for our heart's desire. Sometimes we learn from these painful experiences, but often we don't.

When I was in college I fell in love with a girl none of my friends liked. They tried to tell me I was making a big mistake. I was dismayed. I thought, "My best friends don't like her. What will I do?" I concluded that I needed to find new friends!

Several months later I had to apologize to each of my friends and admit to them that I was temporarily insane. They forgave me, and are still my friends today. Only time heals this kind of wound and shows us that perhaps we had not perceived our own best interests in the situation. I was only considering my own thoughts and what I thought were my needs in the situation and I didn't think of anyone else, not even of the girl I thought I was in love with. I only saw the small picture of my immediate future that I was trying my best to force onto the world. And it wasn't working. I was losing her and I knew it. I could not conceive of a future without her in it, but that was what my future was to be. I had to let the future become what it was to become, dragging me along with it, complaining the whole time. My future, of course, turned out to be much better than anything I could have conceived of.

The disciples had a difficult time with many things Jesus said. In the gospels, the disciples often ask Jesus to explain the meaning of one story or another. They were average people like us, and their own words in the New Testament show this. They saw the small picture but were not so good at seeing the larger vision. For example, they were concerned about what position they held in their master's favor. It was important to them who sat on his left and right, and who was at the end of the table. And like us today, they were not thinking too far beyond their immediate future. But they all wanted things to get better for themselves and Israel and they thought they were associated with the one man who could make it all work. They wanted Jesus to make Israel work, the Israel they knew, right then. Small picture.

As discussed earlier, early Gnostic beliefs included the notion of a secret teaching, something Jesus told only to a few of his disciples. The belief in special teachings and instructions was general at that time. But the idea also could have arisen from those who believed there had to be some kind of hidden meaning or message, in order to make what Jesus said more sensible and more congruent with what actually goes on in the world and to explain why the Kingdom of God hadn't yet arrived. If the disciples didn't understand the teachings themselves, they would have had trouble making the concepts clear to anyone else. Some of the sayings attributed to Jesus in the Gnostic gospels and even in the regular gospels sound much like modern day Zen quotations, which can be nonsensical to those without any knowledge of Zen. An example is, *"Before Abraham was, I am."* This statement also takes us in a direction that questions our understanding of time itself.

We still have trouble believing the simple messages, and we still don't know very much about the Kingdom of God as described by Jesus. How long do we have to wait for the coming of the Kingdom of God with its promise of eternal peace and love? What is salvation? What is eternity? And do we just have to wait or can we actually help it come about?

The whole problem with the end times has to do with time itself. How long is time? And what is eternity? Most have thought of eternity as all of time put together.

I have an interesting very early memory. I was probably about two or three years old. I was looking at the stars and asked my mother how far the stars went. She answered, "They go on forever." I cast my mind out in space as far as I could, then did it again from that point, then again, trying to get to forever. I realized that I couldn't do it, that each mental leap I took left a fence behind me and those fences were limits. This was surprising to me because I remembered a time when I was younger, *when I knew what forever was!* I knew, even then, that forever had no limits. And I also knew, as young as I was, that I had already lost something.

There is an old folk poem that illustrates eternity being all of time:

In the land of Odin, there stands a mountain,
One thousand miles in the air.
Once every hundred years, a tiny bird comes flying by,

And sharpens his beak there.

When the mountain is worn away, this to eternity will be,

Only one single day.

This is a daunting picture, and I don't think Jesus meant for us to look at eternity in that way, although it would explain why the Kingdom of God is a bit tardy.

I think eternity is something else entirely. I think it is the state that exists outside of time. There is no evidence for this in the historical record, of course, because the historical record only shows us what is *in* time. Scholars and scientists who have tackled the question of time just write around it because it is very hard to conceive of anything that does not exist within time and space. We are getting better at this, however. Heaven used to be thought of as a specific physical place, just as hell was supposed to be another physical place deep in the earth. Now people can easily conceive of a spiritual heaven that does not exist on the physical plane. This is one place where science and science fiction have really helped us by constantly expanding the limits of our ability to imagine alternate realities.

Seeing eternity as something outside of time reflects the experience of the mystics. Mystics are people on the edges of all religions. Their experiences are not of this world and not of time itself. The stories they tell are consistent. They have experienced timelessness. They have seen the truth of how everything fits together and how they and everyone else are precious and loved and that there is nothing to fear. When they try to explain their experiences it just sounds like nonsense. It can't be translated into words. It is not rational or scientific. But the experience of the mystics is quite similar to what Jesus described as the pearl of great price, his Kingdom of God.

Bertrand Russell was not a mystic, nor did he believe in mysticism, but he had respect for some of the people who were mystics and he studied the mystical experience. He came up with four common elements. These are:

1. *There is a better way of learning than the senses.*

2. *There is a unity to all things.*

3. *Time is an illusion.*

4. *Evil is only appearance, not reality.* 6

You will notice that the last point is the answer for the *trilemma* mentioned previously, if you substitute the word "suffering" for evil.

Studying time itself is a mysterious and humbling quest. Time becomes strange at the quantum level, where atoms and parts of atoms dance. Physics experiments have shown, and the math agrees, that if we know where something is, we don't know exactly when it is, and vice versa.

On the cosmic level, the theory of relativity has stretched our concept of time. Einstein came up with the theory in 1911 as a young man. Graying scientists all over the world tried to show it was in error. They all failed. The theory of relativity is intact because in a hundred years of effort it hasn't been disproved and all the math still works. The theory predicts that as we go faster, time slows down. When we reach the speed of light, time essentially stops. Astronauts and even airline pilots have proved this to be true in their flights around the earth and to the moon. Time for them did slow down just a bit.

$E=MC^2$, Einstein's famous formula, states eloquently that energy equals mass times the speed of light squared. Even a very small amount of mass, such as a human body, is a tremendous amount of energy if we speed it up—much more energy than is in atomic bombs, which is what most people think the formula describes. An atom bomb only splits the atoms of the heavy, radioactive element Uranium. When the atom splits, the atomic bonds that hold the atom together are broken and this releases some energy, with lighter elements formed as byproducts of the explosion.

$E=MC^2$ means that all mass is actually frozen energy. Since light is energy, it could be said that we are frozen light, waiting to be thawed.

Light is mysterious stuff. You probably remember from high school physics that light can have the properties of either a wave or a particle. A single photon, the smallest increment of light, can be seen by a human eye that has been conditioned to the dark. The interesting thing is, light has two different properties depending upon how we want to see it. If we want to see a particle, light behaves like a particle, but if we want to see a wave, it behaves like a wave. And if we have trouble making up our mind, light will change its behavior to whatever we decide at the moment we decide. *The decision of how light will act is actually faster than the speed of light itself.* This is one of the traits we attribute to consciousness.[7] And if light is this strange, what about time itself?

Some scientists have described these studies as bordering on the religious. Our new picture of time can explain the confusion of the disciples, some of the beliefs of the Gnostics, and the questions that linger about the coming of the Kingdom of God. It would have been extremely hard to explain this alternate view of time to a Hebrew fisherman of two thousand years ago. It is hard to explain today, although we do have the advantage of the expanded vision of science. A hundred years ago, the idea that 300 people could get into an aluminum cylinder and travel half way around the world in a few hours was beyond belief.

So it is probable that Jesus was right all along and the Kingdom of God is imminent and has always been and will always be imminent. Time then becomes the path and method we use in our journey back to our Father's house. With this explanation, the Kingdom of God, salvation, has always been not ahead of us, but right next to us, or even within us. The Kingdom simply awaits for us to decide to mentally sell all we have invested in other things, and finally leave this pigsty and find the one thing in all the world, the one thing that is not of this world, the pearl of great price, which is closer to us than our shadows and waits for us at the end of all roads.

If this picture of eternity is true, or truer than the poem about the mountain and the bird, we can be intentional about seeking the Kingdom of God. When we practice what Jesus said to do, we can be like the mystics. We can have the same experiences of timelessness and eternity that they have. His teachings have just as great an immediacy today. If we do what Jesus said, if we attempt to master the hard lessons of stepping away from blame, judgment, and anger; and if we become the servants of our brothers and sisters without judging their worthiness, we can find the Kingdom of God Jesus said was so close.

The important teachings of Jesus aren't simple aphorisms that will make our lives and relationships easier. In fact, when practiced as he preached, they usually make our lives harder because they force us to move into areas of life and consciousness that directly confront our fears and the general fears of our communities.

"I am sending you out as sheep among the wolves" Jesus told his disciples. As it was then it still is today, which is another reason why so few actually follow his teachings. It is so much easier to participate in meaningless rituals that go back more than a thousand years and pay lip service to the concepts, rather than to actually begin to incorporate what he said.

Jesus' teachings are a systematic practice of non-judgment and forgiveness that is transformative. When practiced, our world actually changes, until we become frightened, and then everything reverts back to the same old world we have always known and feared. We are afraid again, but at least the fears are old and familiar, and therefore less frightening than the unknown.

Becoming fearless is the hardest work there is. But letting go of our fears is the only real work we have to do. We can start doing it now, or we can wait a while longer. The process is as immediate as we choose to make it. I think we literally have all the time in the world.

Conclusion

Two parables and a handful of sayings are at the heart of Jesus' teaching. This is not to say there is less value in the rest of the New Testament. The entire Bible has value on many levels. It is still the best history for the time it was written, and even more importantly, it is one of the earliest and most complete records of mankind's efforts to achieve holiness, to find our way back to God. The Bible is unique in that it accurately describes people, especially rulers, warts and all. I have always been impressed at how honest the Bible is in its description of human frailty. Before the Greeks and Romans, almost all the writing of ancient times glorified and magnified the kings, exaggerating their lives and ignoring their shortcomings. We still see this "leader aggrandizement" in many tyrannical countries like North Korea. The people in the Bible were driven by the same things that drive us today, and they failed just as miserably as we do in getting what they wanted. People haven't changed, not since the beginning of time. We are just the same as those people in Samaria who went out to Jacob's Well to listen to what a new teacher had to say. We want the same things they wanted, and we can learn the same things they learned, if we listen with an open mind.

I have put special emphasis on the two parables and the sayings because they are opposite to the traditional ways of thinking that keep us mired in the world of fear. Our traditional worldly thinking allows us to bring fear into any teaching, no matter how pure. We make mistakes at a prodigious rate, yet we still delight in pointing out the mistakes of others. Nothing we do is perfectly right. Because of this, it matters little whether the source we are considering is free from error or not.

We have enough innate error within us to render perfection unrecognizable, no matter what its form.

People who insist on the perfection and inerrancy of the Bible do so because they think if the Bible contains error, it makes a statement about God, that He is not omnipotent or omniscient. It would mean that if He allowed errors in His words, then somehow He doesn't care for us, or cares for us less. But Jesus told us what to do whenever we think someone else is making a mistake in the way they interpret scripture.

"Why do you observe the splinter in your brother's eye and never notice the plank in your own?"

To insist the Bible is perfect, or to take the opposite view that it is all fiction, is to continue the mistake of the Pharisees. They stood on their principles and pointed out where others were wrong. They were standing on sand. Trying to reconcile all the contradictions, differences, and unanswered questions in the Bible is an impossible dream. Many have tried, but their attempts have never been widely acceptable. The reason is that we interpret things through the unique lens of our own experience and learning. The Bible is a wonderful book, but it is still *just* a book. We give the words meaning by how we choose to read it. Almost any verse can be seen as perfect if we read it through the eyes of love and peace. And the same verse read through the eyes of harsh judgment can be seen as justification for the most heinous crime.

As many as a hundred thousand women in Europe, and more than a dozen in America, were horribly tortured and killed because they were thought to be witches. Many were burned alive at the stake, all because of a single line in the Old Testament: *"You shall not allow a witch to live."* Christians became serial killers on a grand scale doing what they thought was God's work because they interpreted the Bible literally and fearfully. They believed that the devil existed and was working hard to win souls for hell. They believed he had agents in the world helping him and that each lost soul would spend an eternity in the fires of hell. Given these beliefs, finding the agents of hell and nullifying their effect on earth just made good sense. The judges, torturers, jailers and executioners of that time were absolutely convinced they were doing God's work. They were absolutely wrong and became the very devils they most feared. The downward sloping road of fearful judgment always leads to degradation and more suffering, never to happiness.

The basic problem is that whenever we judge, we are wrong. It is the act of judgment itself and not about whatever we are judging, that is the error. If we judge from anger, it is wrong. If we blame others because we think we have been taken advantage of, it is wrong. In any conflict with our brothers or sisters, we are wrong. We cannot judge another as worse than ourselves and still love our brother *as* ourselves. We may be right in seeing that they are in error, but we can be sure that we are more wrong in seeing errors in another.

If you are a normal person you are now thinking of one exception after another of people who really do deserve some kind of retribution for what they did, even if it is only realizing the suffering they have caused.

But there can be no exceptions. Sorry about that. Welcome to the graduate school of forgiveness. Every day is a new class with new lessons and none of us are very good at it, but we can be sure that the lessons will keep on coming.

Jesus said to the mob about to stone an adulteress, *"Let him among you who is without sin cast the first stone."* We are all good at casting stones. Learning to walk around without a stone in our fist is a new experience. Learning that when we throw a stone we only hit ourselves takes even longer.

The Pharisees rejected Jesus and his teachings for good and sound reasons. They saw him as a threat to their religious practices, their culture, and life as they knew it and they were right on all counts. If we really want to follow the teachings of Jesus, we too need to reject all of our traditional thinking and accept a new vision based totally on love and forgiveness. This is no easy task.

We have to give up a great deal. We have to give up our dreams for the things we think will make our lives better, more complete, more safe and secure. But that is just the point. We are giving up old dreams for a new reality that is more real than anything we have yet experienced. It is the pearl of great price, but it is also a pearl we have never seen or even imagined. Having faith means believing that such a pearl exists, and can be found.

The teachings of Jesus don't tell us how to become richer or healthier or wiser or more secure. All these things are of the world and Jesus specifically said his kingdom is not of this world. The teachings of Jesus describe a totally different way of looking at life and the world. His promise is a life totally changed, but his advice is so contrary to the way most people live that following him seems to be impossible. Yet for the past 2000 years, there have been people who have lived their lives in just the way Jesus described, or very close to it, and their examples show that it can be done. Indeed, at some point it must be done. Our only choice is whether to begin now or to walk the fearful path a little longer.

Even when we do decide to make changes, our fears don't suddenly fall away. Some do, but then other fears that have been just under the surface rise up. We have to go through the process again and again and yet again. In order to step away from our fears, we have to see that we have them, and that means that we will continually meet with them until we are ready to let them go. Most of our work has to do with seeing our brothers and sisters as they really are: people just like us who have not let go of their fears.

The parable of the Good Samaritan, along with turning the other cheek to those who attack us, along with treating our neighbors as ourselves—these form the basis of the lesson that every soul on earth, every person who has ever lived, is our brother, our sister, our neighbor.

The way we learn this lesson is to *work* at seeing someone who has betrayed us as a sister or brother. We shouldn't blame people for having fears. Everyone has fears. We shouldn't blame ourselves either. Having let go of fear, we shouldn't blame or judge those who are holding on to the same fears we just relinquished.

The word *sin* taken from the Greek, as used in the New Testament is actually a term from archery and means to miss the bull's eye. We have a tendency to think of sin as something much more serious than that, but all sin is merely a mistake.

The arrow didn't go where we were aiming. We just need to try again. We don't have to be afraid, because all we are doing is missing the mark, which we do continually. It goes without saying that we should not indulge ourselves in criticizing the accuracy of others. We aren't very skilled yet. But skill comes with practice. Eventually we will be able to split our own arrows in the center of the target.

I recently watched a program on TV about hell. It described the many visions and ideas people have had about hell and what the Bible and other religious teachings and traditions say about it. One minister on the program said that he just could not imagine any kind of afterlife where Mother Theresa and Hitler ended up in the same place or were treated the same by God. He said that if he were to believe that he would be outraged at the injustice of it. However, according to Jesus, the way to God is the consciously chosen path of unreasonable, unconditional love, and outrage isn't going to take us there. Outrage only keeps us mired in the world of fear.

Stepping away from our fears is another way we learn to love, and learning to love is what Jesus' ministry was all about. God is the only source of love, so learning love in any form is holy work. Many see love and innocence in children. Some see love when they work with the dying in hospice programs. Some see love in animals of all sorts. Seeing the oneness of God is healing. Seeing the differences and separations of the world is not.

Following the words of Jesus has never been easy. Fearlessness is difficult, and sometimes trying to let go of fear can generate more fear. Whenever we perceive that we have judged harshly, or that we could be more forgiving and should let go of some of our fears, we hear an immediate "Yes, but..." from the part of us that is still firmly fearful. There are always prudent reasons to keep our fears. Letting them go is indeed stepping out in faith.

Many people have managed to follow the teachings of Jesus closely and they are good examples for the rest of us. Mother Theresa of Calcutta had nothing, yet she was richer than anyone. She started her work by simply finding a place where a poor old man could die peacefully and not be alone.

Brother Lawrence, who wrote the letters that became the little book, *The Practice of the Presence of God*, was a Carmelite monk in a monastery in the 17th century. He prayed constantly and simply by turning all his thoughts into a conversation with God. Whatever work he was assigned, he did without question. Every time he failed or felt hurt, he said, "How can I do otherwise if You are not with me?" Every time he succeeded, he gave all the credit to God, saying, "I can do anything with You." He lived in the moment and in such a constant state of peace that others could easily see it.

I have known a few people who carry so much love around with them that others can feel it. In the late seventies I had a construction company in Santa Fe with two partners. One was a Catholic who went to mass regularly and the other was a fundamental Christian. We also had two employees: an expert in Tai Chi and mystical Judaism and a Catholic priest taking a vacation from the Church. Some days when we started talking religion we got very little work done. Those were great days!

The priest was disenchanted with the Church. He had recently returned from an assignment in Rome that had lasted several years. I asked him what he did there and he told me he was in PR. I said, "That sounds like a contradiction in terms," and he replied, "Oh, it is!" But he stayed true to his calling. Even though at that time he had no assignment as a priest, on

Sundays he would drive to one or another Native American Pueblo to say mass and hear confessions. Later he became the Catholic chaplain at the prison in Santa Fe where I used to teach. He also worked doing various priestly things around Santa Fe. He was well aware of the Church's failings. He told me he was one of nine priests currently at the prison, but he was the only one who could go home at night.

My friend continues to serve and he does it well. I spent one Christmas with him a few years ago and was fascinated watching people come and give him little presents and invite him to dinner. They had such love for him. You could see it in their eyes. He was precious to them. Yet he was, and is, unaware that he gives. He loves and it comes back to him, and even if he seems not to see it or feel it, it is there. I know a few people who seem unaware of the good that flows from them and become surprised, and often embarrassed, when someone sees it and points it out.

My daughter Johanna was often sick during her first year. One time she was quite ill with diarrhea and she was unable to keep food down. I was at work and Cherie was home, sitting in the middle of the living room floor with Johanna on a blanket, dirty diapers strewed around her, trying to keep her hydrated with jello water. There was a knock on the door and in came the two Jehovah's Witness ladies who had been visiting regularly. They would come by and talk to Cherie, and sometimes, if I was there, the two of us.

We had told them some of the things that were happening to us and they would read us Bible verses. When they came in that day, Cherie told them, "I'm sorry, my baby is sick. I can't talk today." The women took one look at her and the house and said, "Of course you can't." Then they hung their coats on the coat rack and went to work. With hardly a word spoken, they cleaned the house, did the dishes and a load of laundry, picked up all the dirty diapers and put them in the trash, took the trash outside, made Jello water for Johanna and food for Cherie, put the food and a new box of diapers next to Cherie, then thanked her and left. Johanna turned the corner on her illness and got better shortly after.

There are many examples of such people. Their stories are not hard to find if you look. They come from all the different religions and some have no religion. They emanate a sense of peace and love. Children and animals often feel it. I think these people love without condition, and everything they see falls under this spell of quiet acceptance. All that is necessary is to love God with all our heart, soul and mind, and our brothers like ourselves. This is the original meaning for the word *repent* in both Greek and Hebrew. It isn't a call to feel guilty, or an exhortation to turn away from sin. It is an appeal to turn your whole heart, soul, and mind *toward* God.

No one needs to be gifted to follow this path. In fact, intelligence can often get in the way and act as a barrier to the simple truth. The Pharisees were all intelligent men. *"You must become as a child,"* is in many ways a literal statement, and there are numerous examples.

Doyle Dykes is a well known master guitar player and is also a spokesman for Taylor Guitars. I went to see him when he came to do a clinic at a local guitar store. On the headstock of his personal Taylor guitar was an inlaid white rose. During the clinic he explained why there is a white rose in each of his guitars.

One day he was talking to his young daughter about prayer and told her that in the Bible it says that whenever two or more are gathered together in His name, they can ask for anything. His daughter told him in her evening prayers she asked God for a rose. The next day she asked where it was. Doyle told him that sometimes these things take awhile and told her the next time she prayed to tell God what color rose she wanted. She told her father she wanted a white rose and would pray for that.

The next day Doyle played at a church that had an outreach program for mentally handicapped adults. When he was finished several people came up to him with small presents of food they had grown and made. A little later when he was packing his guitars, a handicapped woman who had not been at the concert came up to him with something wrapped in aluminum foil. She said, "Are you Mr. Dykes?" He said yes, and she said, "God told me to give you this. I got it from the garden." Thinking it was another vegetable, Doyle accepted the package, thanked the woman and told her he would eat it after he got on the road. The woman looked at him strangely and said, "You shouldn't eat it, but God told me to give it to you so you can do what you want." Then she left. Doyle unwrapped the foil to find a single white rose.

I have worked with adults who have mental handicaps from mild to severe. Being unable to read or write does not make these people any less human. Some can exhibit a profound faith. We can learn from all our brothers and sisters, especially those who seem to have less or be less than ourselves.

There are many others who need to be seen through the eyes of forgiveness. A prison is an entire subculture of blame. The blame is supposed to be limited to the inmates because they are the ones found guilty by the courts, but an air of constant suspicion extends through all the staff and to the families who come to visit their relatives. Even trivial mistakes by the staff are met with stern and rapid punishment. Everyone is afraid of what could happen. I spent six years teaching college classes in a prison, and I was surprised at how little difference there was among the convicts inside, the guards watching them, and the people outside. Eventually I found a couple inmates much like myself, who had circumstances only slightly different from my own. A wrong choice here, an unwise habit there, or simply being in the wrong place at the wrong time, was the only difference. Many are just like us, yet the national call of fear (echoed in the cop and crime shows on television) is to put ever more people in prison with longer sentences and more restrictions after they get out. Only then will we feel safe, they tell us. Yet we are more fearful as our prisons grow and more and more money is needed to house this now huge special part of our population.

Jesus compared the human condition to that of a flock of sheep. He said a good shepherd will always look for a single lost sheep. We are all the sheep, and we are all lost. Some of us seem to be more lost than others. Hitler, Stalin, Genghis Khan, Attila the Hun, Herod, and others in history have the label of the worst of sheep, and they were about as lost as sheep can get. Yet, even they are not beyond the pale, if Jesus is to be believed.

The path home to God is simple. We like to see ourselves as complex, but we need to let go of our complexity. We need to have the simple faith of a child, or of the Roman centurion. It isn't difficult in theory; it is difficult in practice.

We have to let go of that part of ourselves that is righteously indignant whenever we judge this or that part of our world to be evil, unfair, cruel, or unloving. The cure for all of this is to love more. We need to see past the lessons of fear and embrace the lessons Jesus taught. Loving our enemies is not an idea we should have a vague admiration for as some kind of cosmic or religious ideal. It is an actual practice that we have to do every waking moment. We have to forgive our enemies by not having any. There are no enemies, only lost sheep, arguing about the best way back to their shepherd. But even while they argue, the shepherd is seeking them so it doesn't matter what path they decide to take because all roads still lead home.

And the kingdom of God? Well, it might very well be closer to you than the end of this book.

Afterword:

The Toy in the Boot

I woke up when the car was skidding sideways. I could hear rocks being thrown up against the wheel wells and undercarriage, and then we were rolling. I was bouncing around inside our small station wagon like a brick in a dryer. I had thought the inside of a car would be softer. It hurt a lot, and I wondered when it would stop because it seemed to go on for a very long time. At one point, I watched my own face rise up from the left, look me in the eye, and then disappear to the right. This didn't seem strange.

The next thing I remember was scrambling out of the open tailgate. The car was upside down. I crawled through a rain of gas from the leaking tank above me. Then there were people around me telling me not to move. I heard Cherie some distance away. I asked the people to help my son, Jesse. I had been asleep in the back of the car with him. We were driving from Santa Fe to Oregon for Christmas with Cherie's family. It was just after sunrise, December 18, 1976, in southern Idaho.

Then Cherie and I were in the ambulance together. I told them to leave me and take Jesse but they didn't. I was in a lot of pain. At the hospital they x-rayed me from every angle, gave me a shot and a neck brace, and told me my son was dead.

Lying on a gurney in the x-ray room, I thought of a dozen things, some going all the way back to my early childhood, that told me I knew this was going to happen. It was very clear that I had always known somehow, that all of my life had been leading up to this moment. But I didn't know I knew. I also had the absolute knowledge that I couldn't have stopped it or changed it, no matter what. This was meant to be. I was told, in a very powerful way I can't explain, that I must never question Cherie's driving or any circumstances leading up to the accident, ever. I never did.

They rolled me into a room with Cherie. I said to her, "Now we only have each other."

Cherie told me, "Jesse woke up an hour before the wreck. He said, 'I am going to be a bird!' And I said, 'Jesse, I don't want you to be a bird. I want you to be a little boy and stay with us.' He said, 'No. I'm going to be a bird. But whenever you want me, you can go out to the apple tree and look up and call, "Jesse! Jesse!" and I'll fly down and be a little boy again.'"

Jesse knew. In the months before his death, he changed from a normal five-year old to someone much older and wiser. Some time in the fall I was reading him some riddles in a children's comic book. Sitting on the fireplace hearth with Cherie, I asked, "What can you hear that makes no sound?" and without a moment's hesitation he said, "My thoughts." I asked, "What can you see that you can't touch?" Again he spoke quickly, "Happiness." The last riddle was, "What can you feel that you can't see?" He looked up at Cherie and me with a big smile and said, "My love for you." I looked at him with wonder and tried to imagine what he was growing to be.

Before he was born I worried about what kind of father I would be, and what kind of changes a child would cause in our lives. Married four years, we were both teaching in the Berkshires in Massachusetts and I was playing in a Bluegrass band at night. I went to the Lamaze childbirth class, and read the books. Cherie was in labor most of the night before waking me at dawn to tell me it was time. I drove her to the hospital, put on a gown, helped her breathe, and held her hand for several hours. After a half hour in the delivery room, Jesse was born. The moment I first saw him, all my questions and fears about what kind of father I would be disappeared. The universe had shifted. From now on my purpose was not to have a life, into which I had to fit a child. Now I had a son, and my new life's purpose was to do anything and everything for him. "Isn't that something!" I thought, with a smile that split my face for the whole day. I went home to tell our friends and family of my new and joyous reduction to servitude.

After the accident, we spent four or five days in the hospital in Burley. We had no broken bones, or cuts, or visible damage. But we walked gingerly, like tentative old people, no longer sure that gravity can be trusted. Our parents had come to be with us. Cherie went into the funeral home to view Jesse's body. I couldn't make myself go. When she got back, she told me that the room was full of light, and she could see that his small body just couldn't hold all that Jesse was now. It gave her a great deal of comfort and peace. My mother told me later that Cherie had stood looking at the small body with a smile on her face, then reached down, as if taking the hand of a child, and said softly, "Come on Jesse. Let's go."

Our parents drove us to the motel Cherie's mother and father owned in the Columbia River gorge. Someone had put a flower arrangement with a lot of red berries on the dresser in our room. Everyone was very nice, their smiles tight and eyes full of concern.

I heard soft plopping sounds that first night. In the morning, when I put on my boots, I discovered the bottom of one was full of berries. During the night, the berries had fallen off the plant and rolled about two to three feet along the dresser top, parallel to the edge, then fell into my boot at the end. I felt really happy for the first time since the wreck. Jesse loved to put things, usually toys, in my boots in the morning. When I put the boot on and ran into the toy, I would shout, and he would dissolve in laughter.

And we stayed on in Oregon for a month before returning to New Mexico. Our house was in Tesuque, just outside Santa Fe, and it was in a shambles because we were in the middle of remodeling. I had stripped the walls and insulated. Only some of the new sheetrock was up. But having the house unfinished actually helped. Our life was undone and it was fitting that our environment reflect this.

We got through the first month because we had a lot of help from family, friends, and neighbors. We found out later that one of our friends had started a large prayer circle out in California that held us in light every day. And we did seem to be almost carried through that time. But when we tried to pick up our routine back in Santa Fe, the real grief came, deep and raw and hard..

We had a stained glass studio on the Plaza in Santa Fe then, so on the bad days we could stay home or go to work, whichever seemed to help the most. But some days it was all we could do just to put one foot in front of the other. One evening I was sitting in my chair with an unread book on my lap, feeling as bad as I had ever felt, when I heard a soft sound from the kitchen. The last thing I wanted to do was to move, but I knew I had to. With the weight of all the world on me, I forced myself up and went into the kitchen. Cherie was huddled in the corner, sobbing quietly. I sat down beside her and held her. There were no words, but it was enough. There is something selfish about grief. It is a dark well, perversely comforting to go down into alone. But I knew that if I stayed there, I would somehow be lost. Death is the flat statement of no hope and that we are truly alone. To deny this, and to heal, we have to reach out to another.

Before Jesse died, Cherie and I were agnostics. But his death gave us several things, several certainties, that we could build on. One was that while he was dead, he wasn't gone. Something of him was still with us; something more than memory or wishful thinking; something solid and real. That meant that I had been wrong. We do have souls, and death isn't a final end.

We had known on some level that this was coming and we soon learned that others knew also. A college friend of ours had a Tarot Card reading from her grandmother. The reading said a child would die, close to you but not close, and it happens in sevens. The accident was seven months after the reading, seven days before Christmas, and the car rolled over seven times. This friend and her husband were the only people we knew in Idaho, and they helped us in the days after the wreck, and told us of the reading. That meant to me that some kind of plan was being worked out, and we were part of it. I knew somehow that Jesse died for me. I didn't know why, but I knew it was so, and I knew it was important.

We had close friends I thought would help us a great deal, who were of no help at all, and acquaintances who turned out to have an inner strength that amazed us and were only too happy to share it. Nothing was as I imagined it would be. No amount of planning would have helped at all.

Friends had offered to come to our house and put away all of Jesse's toys and things. They said it would be better than coming back to a house full of reminders. We decided to do it ourselves but it didn't help. Coming home to the toys Jesse would never touch again was hard, but so was not having them. One morning Cherie and I were having breakfast and talking about the day. I reached down and put one boot on, and was pulling on the other when my toe hit something. Without a word I took off my boot and held it up to Cherie, then turned it over. A little car fell out into my hand. The house had been clear of toys for a month. It felt like the morning sunlight in the kitchen doubled.

After a great loss, a lot of what people tell you is bad advice, but they mean well. In our grief, we had a heightened sensitivity to feelings. People would say truly awful things to us like, "You aren't going to have another child are you? You know you can't replace him." But we could clearly see the pain they felt for us, and the hard effort they were making to somehow connect and say something, anything, to make us feel better or avoid further pain. There was nothing to forgive because we could see they loved us and were doing the best they could.

That first year after Jesse's death was very hard, yet also wonderful. We had dozens of experiences like finding the toy in the boot. Some were reminders like the toy, telling us that the world really isn't as it appears, and others showed us to pay closer attention to the people around us. Sometimes attention can make all the difference. Love and kindness are the antidotes for loss and we often found it in unexpected places. One night Cherie and I were shopping in Penney's. We were waiting behind a couple at the cash register. The clerk, an older woman, was having trouble. She kept making mistakes and it took her some time to get it right. The couple was irritated and walked away indignantly.

The woman took a deep breath, smiled, and asked if she could help us. Cherie had been watching her closely, and she knew that something was off. Touching her hand Cherie asked, "Are you all right?" The woman smiled again and said, "Oh yes." But then her face crumpled and she started crying. "No I'm not! My son died last week and *I don't know what I'm doing!*"

We knew just how she felt, bravely trying to go through the motions of normality when it seemed that everything of real value and meaning has been taken away. We talked with her for fifteen or twenty minutes, and we cried together. I told her about the toy in the boot. Every other customer in the store went somewhere else for that time. We were like three people on an island. When we left we knew she had the strength to meet another hour, maybe another day or week, and we were stronger too.

Everything seemed to be leading us toward church, and when we eventually did go, the Sunday after Easter, we found it a great comfort. The hymns and sermons seemed to be directed right to us. When I was in junior high there was a Baptist church across the street from the school with a neon sign on the side that said, "Christ died for you." I never understood that but now I was starting to get the idea.

Tesuque is a lovely little valley with a small river running through it. There are beautiful black-and-white magpies and large flocks of several hundred big gray birds that eat the piñon pine tree nuts in the surrounding hills. One cold afternoon I was working outside, sanding boards that were going to be the wainscoting for our living room. The boards were rough-sawn timber from the sawmill. I had cut them to size, and was sanding them smooth. I was intent, because if you aren't focused with power tools you endanger the wood and yourself. This was repetitive, boring work, and I was talking to myself. I had taught myself the art of stained glass and now I was learning how to build a house. "Well here I am, the carpenter." I said. "Just like Jesus, except I've got a belt sander."

What happened next will stay with me always. One of the large flocks of birds was overhead. I was not aware of them; the sander made a lot of noise and my eyes were on the workbench. As I spoke the last word, the entire flock dived down and surrounded me. They were flying all around me, inches from my face, under my legs and arms, around and around me they flew, a swirling avian caress, then up and away off to the east and the mountains. I watched the flock until it was just a small darkening in the late winter sky, then carefully put the silent sander down, and walked under the apple tree at the corner of the house to tell Cherie.

We usually don't know how the things we say and do affect others over the long term, but every now and then, something comes back. We never saw the woman in Penney's again. I told the story of the toy in the boot in public only once. Writing it now is the second time I have told the story to more than one or two people.

The inspirational author Hugh Prather is a friend of mine. Cherie and I met him and his wife Gayle when they wanted stained glass windows for the house they were building in the early seventies. In 1981 Hugh started a new church in Santa Fe, and as soon as I heard about it, we went. The church met at the Girl's Club, and they didn't have anybody to play music. I brought my guitar the next Sunday, and ended up taking care of most of the music from then on. It was in that church that I found I could begin writing songs about my experiences, six years after Jesse's death.

In the summer of 1982, Hugh and his friend Jerry Jampolsky went to Atlanta to help the parents of the slain children when the serial killer was on the loose there. Hugh asked me to talk on the Sunday he would be gone, and to just tell about Jesse's death, and all that came from it. Hugh was popular in Santa Fe. Most of the congregation knew he was gone and stayed home. One woman had come all the way from San Francisco to hear Hugh. When she found he wouldn't be speaking she was dismayed and almost left. She again thought of leaving when she learned I would be talking about the death of my child. Against her better judgment, she stayed.

When she got back to California, she told a friend the story of the toy in the boot. Some time later that friend called her with the terrible news that her son had just committed suicide. "I want you to know," she said, "that the *only* thing keeping me alive right now is that story you told me of the toy in the boot."

I didn't find out about this until ten years later. I was asked to speak at another church. The woman who introduced me was the same one who stayed years before. She is a therapist and for years has used the story in her work, sharing it with thousands of people.

The unusual happenings occurred less often after that first year. They were our lifeline when we were so fragile. Our daughter was born a little less than a month before the anniversary of Jesse's death and our second daughter two years later. They are the lights of my life.

I remember a quote from one of the many religious books I read back then: "Every bush is a burning bush, if we but have the eyes to see." The world tells us love is a rare and fleeting thing, hard to find, and even harder to keep. In a verse in one of my songs I wrote, "They leave us, on a lonely road. And the armor I wear, is full of holes." But there is another reality, very close to us, where love heals everything.

I still watch the birds and listen for the song behind the world I see. There is a plan and I am part of it. We are all part of it. Jesse showed me.

A Simple Guide to "Practicing Jesus"

God loves you. He always has and always will. You are precious to Him. Nothing you have ever done or will ever do will change this. He is looking for you now and wants you to come home. He needs you.

All people are beloved children of God. See no differences among them.

Love your enemies because God loves them as much as He loves you. It is *not* necessary to first try to explain why He loves them. Just do it.

There is nothing to fear. Not now, not tomorrow, not ever.

When we are angry, we are always wrong. Let it go.

Don't attack others in thought or action.

When attacked, don't defend yourself.

Question all conventional wisdom silently to yourself.

Assume that you know less, and are therefore farther from the truth, than everyone else on earth, and they are the only ones who can show you what and where the truth is.

Listen carefully to what they say and make the effort to agree with them twice, before you state your mind.

When listening, notice that with every exchange you have with other people in the world, only one of two things is happening. The other person is either giving you some kind of an expression of love, or they are asking for an expression of love for themselves from you. Expressions of anger and fear are always a call for love.

Return expressions of fear with expressions of love, and give thanks whenever you receive the gift of love.

Look for simple solutions for immediate needs.

Be aware that anything can happen at any time.

Love without reservation. Everyone else is just as afraid as you, although some are better at hiding it. When you love, it allows everyone else to fear less.

When in despair, look around. Someone nearby may need a hand.

Remember there are no sins, only mistakes, and everyone makes mistakes—all the time.

Be fearless, because at this moment, right now, there is nothing to fear, and this moment, right now, is all that matters. Don't worry about tomorrow.

Spend time each day thinking about love.

When you practice love and forgiveness, you will find the pearl of great price.

When trying to find the right religion, denomination, path or practice to follow, do not vex yourself. It is unnecessary because of the one common element in all the beliefs of the world, which is you, the believer. Those who believe, the pilgrims, the lost sheep trying to find their way home, are not made better by the religion or the belief or even the lack of belief they profess, rather it is their own innate holiness and the grace we all carry within, that does the work. This is why those who practice beliefs with no history or even coherent methodology are helped and satisfied by their experience. No matter what path we choose, it is our own holiness that lights our way and will ultimately guarantee our journey. This is what Jesus meant when he said, "Your faith has healed you."

Footnotes

1 Nevil Shute, <u>Slide Rule-The Autobiography of an Engineer,</u> William Heinemann, (1954) pp 190-192

2 Tony Hillerman, <u>People of the Darkness,</u> Harper Paperbacks, 1980 pp 262-263

3 Paul Ilton, <u>The Bible Was my Treasure Map,</u> Julian Messner, Inc., NY, 1958, pp55

4 The Biblical Archeological Review (all issues 2007-2012)

5 Steve Mason, <u>Josephus and the New Testament,</u> Second Ed., Hendrickson Pub., Peabody, MA, 2003 pp

6 Bertrand Russell, *Mysticism and Logic and Other Essays*, London: Longmans, Green and Col, 1925, as cited in <u>The Medium, the Mystic, and the Physicist,</u> Lawrence LeShan, Penquin/Arkana, NY, 1974, pp43

7 Gary Zukav, <u>The Dancing Wu Li Masters,</u> <u>An Overview of the New Physics,</u> Bantam Books, NY,1979 pp 62-63

Notes on the Sayings

If you do a search using the sayings of Jesus that I used in this book, you won't find them in any Bible. I used the online parallel bible to see what all the different translations were. They had a tendency to clump together. Many follow or are improvements on the King James version, but in those the language tends to be too archaic. In others there is still a tendency to make the language something other than the everyday speech Jesus would have used with his companions and followers. I have read that when something is translated from one language to another, with each word there is a possible choice of six words and finding just the right one that will keep the original meaning intact is not an easy job. So with the sayings in this book, I made my own translations. If you question my method, I urge you to do it yourself and come up with your own. It did make me feel closer to the original teachings.

Bibliography

Hillerman, *Tony. People of the Darkness. New York, 1980.*

Hoffer, Eric. *The True Believer: Thoughts on the Nature of Mass Movements.* New York: Harper Classics, 1951.

Huntress, Keith. *Murder of an American Prophet: Joseph Smith, 1805-1844.* San Francisco: Chandler Publishing, 1960.

Ilton, Paul. *The Bible Was My Treasure Map.* New York: Julian Messner, Inc., 1958.

LeShan, Lawrence. *The Medium, The Mystic, and the Physicist: Toward a General Theory of the Paranormal.* New York: Penguin/Arkana, 1974.

Lewis, C.S.. *Mere Christianity.* San Francisco: Harper, 1952.

_____. *The Great Divorce.* New Jersey: Prentice Hall, 1978.

Mason, Steve. *Josephus and the New Testament.* Peabody: Hendrickson Publishers, 2002.

Shute, Nevil. *Slide Rule: The Autobiography of an Engineer.* London: Heinemann, 1954

_____. *Round The Bend.* London: Heinemann, 1951.

_____. *The Chequer Board.* London: Heinemann, 1947.

The Biblical Archaeological Review. Washington, DC: Biblical Archaeological Society.

Biography

Jonathan Huntress has worked as a musician, teacher, stained glass artist, contractor, minister, journalist, and writer. But his life changed dramatically in 1976 when his son was killed in an automobile accident. Before that event, Jonathan was a free thinking agnostic, but his son's death and what followed forcefully changed his mind. When his friend Hugh Prather started a non-denominational church in Santa Fe a few years later, Jonathan provided the music and later became a minister for the church. He has masters degrees in History, Special Education, and Computer Information Systems. His book *Tis The Gift to be Simple* reveals a lifetime of intense study and contemplation on the subject of Jesus and the history that surrounds him. More importantly, it shows how we can change our own world by simply changing our mind about the way we see it.